Wh

Go..., -

The important power of the book is the first person narrative and how Jan's faith has grown and matured throughout the ordeal and her subsequent life with her husband. I was most intrigued by the whole story and the details of her varied and adventurous life. I know that this book will bless many people particularly those who are going through a grieving time.

...Dr. Vic Casad, Senior Pastor,
Stonebridge United Methodist Church, McKinney, Texas

~~~

I began reading Jan's account of the tragic loss of her family with great trepidation. As an active duty Air Force officer, I had just begun my journey home from a year-long assignment in Korea and absence from my own family. The two events occurred almost simultaneously. My reunion with my family was such a joyful event as compared to the unimaginable grief in Jan's life.

Jan's family and mine had been close since our parents were young. I had literally known her all of her life. My initial emotion was one of intense hatred for the man who caused this tragedy followed by a bewildering disbelief at how God could have allowed this to happen. Although diminishing with time, I continued to harbor these feelings throughout the years. Only by reading Jan's book have I fully been able to grasp the true meaning of letting things go and trusting in God's plan. If Jan could cope with what was dealt to her, then surely the petty inconveniences in my life can be understood. As I finished reading Jan's book, I felt my trepidation turn to a peaceful understanding.

...John Roane, Cooke County Judge,
Gainesville, Texas

~~~

Wow…I swallowed each word quickly like a starving man, and then I too soon came to the end and clamored to read more and more. Everyone that loves Jan has longed to hear the untold story of that fateful day, to share that which only she and God have shared for years now. Thank you for reaching deep within and pulling back memories that must still cut to your very soul.

…Lisa, author's sister

~~~

This book is an incredible message of grace, compassion, faith, and love! Jan and I worked together during my tenure as Pastor at Nocona Hills Community Church. She had an amazing ministry gift of compassion toward the hurting and was always willing to pour herself out to others spiritually. This book helped me to understand where that gift and anointing came from. Her relationship with the Savior is genuine and refreshingly rare. Tragedy leaves most people bitter and antagonistic toward God, but because of her relationship with Him, her attitude and heart is a perfect example of what it means to be Christ-like. I wept, I laughed, and I rejoiced as I read this incredible story of a real life tragedy that somehow became a testimony of victory. It made me desire to know Him in a much deeper and intimate way. Great work Jan! Thanks for obeying His voice by sharing God's never ending grace and love with us! Everyone should read it!

…Joseph Jernigan, Jr., former Pastor,
Nocona Hills Community Church, Nocona, TX

~~~

It's such a 'personal' story of courage and faith…but written in a way that everyone can relate to. One of the things I came away with is a renewed feeling of just how each moment of our lives is a blessing…precious and so fragile.

…Judy, author's treasured friend

~~~

In *God, Help Me!*, Jan shares honestly and openly about her struggle during her time of unimaginable crisis. Her account of how God brought her through to victory is what is needed for those who find themselves on the same journey. Reading and sharing her story certainly will make the burdens we face during extreme crisis more bearable.

...Dan Sanders, retired Pastor,
Centerpoint Church, Pagosa Springs, CO

~~~

God, Help Me! is a well written book that will reach out to help anyone through difficult situations; showing how through our faith, the Spirit can speak for us when the words are not there. I believe anyone reading this book will be enlightened to God's power.

...Cecilia Langley, Nocona Hills Community Church
Women's Ministry, Nocona, Texas

~~~

From the moment I heard of Jan's accident, I felt immense sorrow for her loss. God's actions brought us together in a deep friendship that blossomed into a new joyful life for us in marriage. From the beginning of our relationship, I realized she was a strong, mature, blessed woman who had endured and found strength in her Lord. She has led me closer to God as I lived and learned from her journey. In writing this book, Jan has displayed an amazing amount of courage as she opened her soul to others. I am extremely proud of the way she has responded to God's callings.

...Bob, author's husband

GOD,
HELP ME!

Janice Anderson

CROSSBOOKS·
PUBLISHING

CrossBooks™
A Division of LifeWay
1663 Liberty Drive
Bloomington, IN 47403
www.crossbooks.com
Phone: 1-866-879-0502

First published by CrossBooks 8/15/2012

ISBN: 978-1-4627-1964-8 (sc)
ISBN: 978-1-4627-1966-2 (hc)
ISBN: 978-1-4627-1965-5 (e)

Library of Congress Control Number: 2012911420

Printed in the United States of America

This book is printed on acid-free paper.

People can never predict when hard times might come.
Like fish in a net or birds in a trap,
people are caught by sudden tragedy.
—Ecclesiastes 9:11–12

~~~

Look! I am making everything new.
Write it all down—each word dependable and accurate.
—Revelation 21:5

DEDICATION

I dedicate this book and my life with deep gratitude and affection to my spiritual Father, the Lord Jesus Christ. Everything I am and everything I will ever be, I owe to Him.

~~~

To my loving husband, Bob, the light of my day. The love we share is a precious gift from God. Thank you for your patience, respect, tenderness, love and especially for the encouragement to step out of my comfort zone and share my story.

~~~

To my cherished support group of family and friends, who served as vessels through whom God worked His amazing healing power. Living my life without all the love and support each of you provided throughout the years would have been impossible. Words cannot express the overwhelming appreciation I have for each of you. God used each one of you individually to fill an enormous void in my life, helping me to recover, grow and flourish in my new life. Thank you for being there when I needed you most, but more importantly thank you for continuing to be my family in Christ.

TABLE OF CONTENTS

PREFACE

In *God, Help Me!*, I share the catastrophic loss and recovery transformation I endured during my life. I offer details of what grew out of my own experiences. Through my learned knowledge, I discovered loss did not define who I am, but how I responded to the loss that mattered. All through the years, people have asked me, "How did you survive the devastation in your life?" I typically answered their question with one word, "God." God saved me all right, but the answer is so much more complicated.

Twenty-five years later, God has now directed me to answer this question in more detail and place my experiences, as best I can remember, into this book. In it, I share my most intimate, private thoughts and prayers in an effort to communicate the personal relationship I developed with God in order to survive. Once I began reminiscing and writing about my life, a new world opened up to me. I asked myself new questions and ultimately found the answers to be unsettling, yet satisfying.

I called out to God as my world around me was shattered. In order to hear God answer me, my faith had to be strengthened, but more importantly, I had to learn to listen. He spoke softly, tenderly and gently to me. My own experiences taught me to understand that the choices we make every day define who we are as a person. God gave me difficult choices at times, but ultimately I chose joyfulness to define myself.

The purpose in passing on my story is not to provide a quick or painless solution to those experiencing loss or difficult times, but to point the way to a lifelong journey of growth in God's love. I do not claim to have all the answers, nor will I say the passage will be effortless. I am merely sharing with you how I survived through God's amazing grace and mercy. I pray each of you will understand that finding joy in each day will set us free and give us peace regardless of the battles being fought in our lives.

May God bless each of you in this season of your life and may you find protection, favor and grace through our Lord Jesus Christ.

CHAPTER 1

Saturday, July 5, 1986

The smell … I remember the smell. It was the smell of hot radiator fluid, that kind of chemical, steamy, hot metal smell. I couldn't move. I was trapped, upside down, and I immediately felt the intense heat of the July day. As I became more aware of my surroundings, the pain began to force itself into my body. My heart began to race as I realized that I was in excruciating pain. I was able to free my right arm just enough to touch my lower abdomen where I felt the concentration of pain. I felt something stretched taut across me; it was my lap belt holding me tightly against the seat. I felt something running down my left cheek. I touched my face and brought my hand in front of my eyes. I felt and saw a sticky, thick, red liquid that dripped from my cheek. Then I could taste the blood. I lay there frightened, wondering what had just happened.

I heard nothing, except for the steam escaping from an engine. There were no cries for help—just a terrifying void, a silence. I began to come to the awareness that I was trapped and badly injured. Then it all began coming back to me. I had been with my family returning home from our vacation. My family! What about my husband and two children? Why

1

couldn't I hear them? Why weren't they screaming out for help? I cried out for my husband, Larry, but there was no answer. I thought about my precious firstborn, who was ten years old, and called out for my blue-eyed, blond-haired son, Cliff. I still heard no answer. I thought about my darling eight-year-old daughter, who had been lying in the backseat asleep just moments before, exhausted from our weeklong campout. Her long, curly brown hair was wet, as was the new pink swimsuit she still wore. She had begged to swim one more time in the lake before we started the long drive home. I called out Adrianne's name, but for the third time, there was only silence—an eerie, deafening silence. There was that smell again! I knew that what I smelled, and the silence I heard, were my senses telling me death was all around me.

What had happened? Was I already dead or slowly dying? Maybe this was all a dreadful nightmare … but no, I knew better. I knew in my heart, at that very instant, my husband of thirteen years and my two precious children were gone. For some unknown reason, I was still alive. I lay bleeding, hurting, and trapped in a pile of crumpled, heavy, hot metal. I couldn't move, and I was becoming weaker every second. Without another thought, I cried out to the only one who could help me. I shouted aloud, "God, help me!" The open wounds on my face began to sting as tears, mixed with the blood, began to run down my face. Then the blackness came.

A loud brash voice, a man's voice, awakened me, saying, "Goddamn it! All the bastards are dead!"

I wasn't dead! I heard another person. I wanted to say, "Wait, I'm still alive, help me!" I tried calling out to him, but I was so weak I couldn't make him hear me—or maybe he didn't want to hear me. Again, there was silence. Sometime later, I learned from witnesses that this man had caused the wreck. He left my family and me in the wreckage and drove away in his truck to discard his beer cans in a ditch along the road, giving himself time to sober up before the police arrived. How could anyone be so coldhearted to run away from the sight that was before his eyes? What kind of person was this? He was cursing the same God I had called out to in a desperate prayer for help just moments before.

I lay there in darkness, drifting in and out of consciousness. I awoke again to the saintly voices of people as they offered their help. I heard them calling out to discover if anyone was alive in the vehicle. I cried out for them to help me. They began speaking to me, telling me help was on the way. They began trying to get me out of the wreckage, but the crushed mass of metal surrounding me was too much for their bare hands.

It wasn't long until I heard the blessed sound of paramedics. I heard the sound of metal being cut and pulled away. As they removed it, the movement caused me to cry out from the agonizing pain. The paramedics kept speaking to me until they had me free from the debris. But why was I still hurting when they had me out of our vehicle? My head pounded as they placed my neck in a brace. I fought back the tears of pain when they lifted the cool, hard stretcher and began to roll me away from the wreck.

Once I was inside the ambulance, the medics immediately began treatment. They placed an oxygen mask over the bleeding wounds on my face. I felt the prick of a needle as an EMT inserted an IV. As my eyes darted about trying to recognize what was happening, I heard a female voice tell the driver, "Go, go, go!" The big, heavy doors slammed closed, only to open again as the EMTs helped someone else into the ambulance. Out of the corner of my eye, I could see a man sitting across from me on a bench, but I didn't recognize him. The medics continued to work on me. It was all so surreal. I felt as if I were undergoing some sort of out-of-body experience watching the scene unfold.

The injured man began complaining to the paramedics. He was cursing, saying he was hurting and that he needed help. The female EMT attending to me forcefully told him, "Shut up!" She said, "You only have a leg injury, and this woman is in serious condition." Whom was she talking about? He persistently cursed and complained about his own pain, the roughness of the road, and the length of time it was taking to arrive at the hospital.

I continued floating in and out, only awakened at times by hands shaking me, telling me to stay with them. Why wouldn't she let me sleep? I felt so much better there. I wasn't even certain I wanted to stay with them. Was there another place better for me, possibly the place where my husband and children had been taken—a place with no pain or crying, a place of peace?

I was unaware when we arrived at the hospital. I awoke to an intensely bright light glaring over my head, and I felt nurses with scissors cutting through all my clothing. Where was I? What was happening? Everyone was in such a hurry. The nurses began questioning me about whom they could call. I told them we had just left my aunt and that they could call her. One nurse asked for her phone number, and I was coherent enough to tell her where it was located in my purse. I'm not sure why I didn't tell them to call my parents, but in all the confusion, I believed we weren't far from where my aunt lived, when in fact we had traveled well over an hour away from her home.

I was somewhat aware of my surroundings, but feeling as if I were in a dreamlike state. I cried and begged the nurses to give me something for the pain, but they told me they couldn't until they knew the extent of my injuries. A man in a white jacket held a clipboard and pen in front of me and told me he was a doctor and he needed to do surgery. He was requiring me to sign a release before he could do anything. I told him I wanted to wait to sign until my aunt was with me. She was a registered nurse, and I felt she would know if I really needed the surgery. I had never had an operation. Maybe I really didn't need one. How could I know for sure? I was confused, scared, and hurting. I didn't know what was happening. I wanted someone I knew and trusted with me before I could make such a decision.

Nurses attended to me constantly, and then I realized they were beginning to shuffle around even more quickly than before. The nurses suddenly became frantic and started shouting, "We're losing her!" The doctor was in front of me again, but this time he told me he couldn't wait for anyone to arrive, he needed to do surgery immediately, or I would die. Again, he placed the pen in my hand, pointed to a line on the paper, and pleaded with me to sign. I signed, trusting a man whom I had never before seen.

I lay helpless, depending on strangers to save my life. I closed my eyes and began to pray silently that God would rescue me from the darkness I felt creeping into me. More than mere humans needed to save me. I needed saving not only physically, but also emotionally and spiritually. I needed the one who could perform these miracles—my God.

I knew I had to pray for help. But what should I ask? In the Bible, the apostle Paul explains to us that we do not have to get down on our knees and repeat a formal prayer for God to hear us; we simply need to ask the Holy Spirit for help. Paul says if we are not sure what we need to ask for in our time of weakness, the Holy Spirit will pray for us, speaking to God with a groaning not expressed in a language that we can even hear or understand. I wasn't even sure I wanted medical help; maybe it would be best if I joined my family. At that very moment, I knew I was definitely at the lowest, weakest point of my life.

I believe with all my heart and soul, while I laid in the mangled metal of our vehicle on a lonely stretch of road somewhere in southeastern Oklahoma, the very moment I cried out asking God to help me, the Holy Spirit recognized my need and instantly summoned God's help. From that point on, unbeknownst to me, God would guide the rest of my life. It would take many years to understand the events that transpired that day and the future God had in store for me.

It is said we should pray without ceasing, and that is what I began doing. I prayed every moment of every day; my life became a constant prayer. I did not know what to ask for; I simply asked God to treat me as the empty vessel that I was and fill me with the Holy Spirit's power and inspiration.

CHAPTER 2

Gifts of Love

In the Bible, a gift is defined as "a noun,
a present from people to people;
a sacrifice from people to God;
anything given voluntarily;
that which is given from God,
which enables or empowers His people to give to others."

I awoke the next morning in ICU feeling agonizing pain throughout my body. As I managed to open my eyes and look through the dried blood in my lashes, the first thing I saw was Mother, Daddy, and my oldest brother standing over me, tears flowing from their reddened eyes. I immediately felt our love exchanged through the look in their eyes and their gentle touches. I was unable to carry on a conversation, but knowing they were with me was such a comfort. The first gift I received that day was that I was still alive, but I quickly recognized coming in a close second was the gift of a loving family, a gift from God for which I am and will always be eternally grateful.

Other family members took turns coming into my room. They were crying and lovingly touching me. My husband's parents and his only sibling, his brother, came in, and I felt their love for me, but I also felt a tremendous sorrow for them as they had suffered a devastating loss in their family as well. I had known Larry and his family since their move to my hometown more than twenty years before. Larry and I were sixth grade classmates that year, and his dad was the head coach in our small school. Now his family stood beside me, arms intertwined, shocked, and distraught having just hours before learned of the death of their only other child, their youngest son and their only two grandchildren. I look back now and understand the enormously overwhelming devastation they must have felt at that moment.

The drugs continued to keep me comfortable as I drifted in and out of a drug-induced state. No one spoke to me regarding the wreck or the fact my husband and children were gone, but then there was really no need for discussion. My parents told me later the doctor had instructed them not to discuss the deaths with me, when I was ready to know, I would ask. But there was no need for me to ask anyone. I had known since the moment I called out for Larry, Cliff, and Adrianne while I lay in the wreckage.

I knew they were gone. Yet I had a peace about me, a strange kind of peace—a peace I had never known before in my thirty-two years. Sometime later, when I told others how I felt that day, they jokingly responded it was probably the drugs. But I know in my heart and soul no manufactured medication can give anyone the kind of peace with which God blessed me during this time. He demonstrated to me the love He has for all His children and how He will take care of us if we will only ask and allow Him to do so. I felt as a small child would feel while being held in her mother's arms after being injured. I felt protected and safe, as if everything was going to be all right.

~~~

Time was elusive; days and nights ran together. Doctors, nurses, family, and others came in and out of my room. I rarely spoke to anyone, but we shared the pain without exchanging a word.

Psalm 37:6–8 says, "Be still in the presence of the Lord, and wait patiently for Him to act." I understand now that when we are placed into certain situations and are at a loss for words, it may be God's way of telling us to *be quiet and just listen.* Sometimes the *less* we speak, the more we *say.* Be still and let God's presence comfort those in need by working through their eyes, their touch, and their silent tears.

My parents were devastated; they could scarcely function. After the hospital contacted my aunt, my uncle had been the one to call my parents to inform them of the wreck, my condition, and the loss of their son-in-law and two grandchildren. My mother collapsed upon hearing the news. My brother, David, who is twelve years older than I am, was the one my daddy called to drive them to the hospital two hours away. Danny, my only other brother, who is ten years older than I am, immediately flew in from his home in Michigan to be with our family. My sister, Lisa, who is four years younger than I am, came as quickly as she could from her home in St. Louis. The three of them took care of my every need and those of our parents, each one dealing with the circumstances the best way he or she knew how.

David became the one who managed my business affairs that needed attention. He began piecing together information regarding my medical insurance and meager finances. David and his wife, Marcia, were the ones who began making funeral arrangements for my family. It must have been tremendously difficult for David to approach me the first time, especially since no one had really spoken to me about the deaths. God was certainly working through David during this time. He dealt with his responsibilities by means of strength beyond any power he had ever known or experienced.

I was completely unprepared for the questions David began to ask. Larry and I had never discussed our desires for our own funerals. However, when David began to ask me where I wanted to have the funerals, what hymns I wanted sung, and if there was someone I wanted to sing them, the reality struck me hard, and I began to answer his questions methodically one by one.

The first song that came to mind was one of Larry's favorites and mine. He would occasionally sing for me in his beautiful, deep soulful voice as he strummed his guitar, "Oh Lord, my God, when I in awesome wonder, consider all the things thy hands have made, how great thou art." There was a man who had sung this beautiful song solo in my church throughout my youth. He also sang at our wedding thirteen years before, so it seemed natural that he be the one to sing at Larry's funeral. David suggested we have just one service for the three family members. I agreed, thinking I would certainly want them to all be together during such a dreadful time. I continually broke down emotionally, and it rapidly became obvious this was too overwhelming for me to handle. Thankfully, David completed the remainder of the arrangements.

The discussion of funeral arrangements brought the sudden realization that I did not have the money to pay for one funeral, let alone three. Almost simultaneously to my thought, David told me not to worry about the cost of the funerals. He said the funeral home director informed him that someone had requested all the bills for the funerals be sent directly to him or her and had asked for anonymity.

Tears flooded my eyes, and suddenly there within me was the peaceful feeling again. "But when you give to someone in need, don't let your left hand know what your right hand is doing. Give your gifts in private, your Father, who sees everything, will reward you" (Matthew 6:3–4). My mind raced as I wondered who could be so generous to give such a precious contribution, it was certainly another gift from God! I praised God and prayed He would bless the person He had *empowered* with the funds to give such a treasured gift.

Minutes, hours, and days passed as I lay in the bed with bandages on my face and head, clumps of dried blood and glass in my hair, and tubes inserted all over my body. For years to come, minuscule pieces of glass would continue to work their way out of the scars on my face. They became constant reminders, like memories, which would come to the surface of my soul. Machines beeped and lights flashed every few seconds while I lay secluded in that small, stark room, barren of any decor or color.

Visitors and mourners would come and go, some of whom I did not even recognize or know. I do remember my boss from Wichita Falls coming to see me. He stood nervously next to me, tears in his eyes, and then he picked up my hand, bent over, and gently kissed it. He was there for only a few minutes, but for some reason, I remember wondering why he had driven over three hours to stand next to me for only a short time.

My brother, Danny, took over much of the personal aspects of the situation. He kept a log of the day, time, and name of every person who called or came to visit. My parents told me later he never left my side. I particularly remember one instance about Danny being there, and it still brings a smile to my face. The nurses had begun delivering me meals; well, essentially the meals consisted of Jello and broth. After several of these liquid delicacies, one day I made a casual comment to Danny about how I wished they would stop bringing me green Jello because I had never liked anything but red. He instantly scooped the bowl of wiggly green stuff off my tray and marched out to the nurse's station, where he emphatically informed the nurses that from then on I was to receive only red Jello.

Family members who were sitting near the nurses' station told me later that Danny didn't exactly say it that nicely. No matter how he said it, I will never forget the love I had for him when he came back into my room, sat down, and, with a sheepish grin on his face, told me the nurses were going to bring me red Jello. It's hard to believe a simple thing like the color of Jello can enrich a sibling relationship!

My sister, Lisa, who had a very young family herself, strengthened me with emotional support. Being my closest sibling, she and I always did and will have a special bond. Words did not need to be spoken between us; we had always known what the other felt. However, I knew in my heart that she did not know the feelings I was experiencing at this time. Still, she would come into my room, sit, and smile with silent tears rolling down her cheeks. And as a mother would do, she would gently pat my hand, expressing the comfort she knew. That was all I needed from her at that moment, to know she was there with me and that she cared. I learned an important lesson through this experience with Lisa—sometimes all it takes are "just tears" to offer the compassion and grief to show someone we care.

Word of the wreck spread to friends who had been members of our church and personal family friends for many years. They were on a family vacation in their motor home. (A year or so before, this family had tragically lost their oldest son when a drunk driver hit him.) This family immediately returned from their vacation, parked their motor home in the hospital parking lot, and kept it stocked with food, supplies, and anything else my family needed. Their unselfish actions provided my family a much-needed refuge from the hospital surroundings and gave them a place for solitude. What a generous and unselfish family to sacrifice their vacation time to care for their friends.

Anyone who has spent any time caring for someone in the hospital and sleeping in a chair knows what a blessing something as simple as a nearby bed can be. This generous gift taught me a lesson of how important it is to think of ways to help those in need and take action to ensure their needs are met. If our friends had asked my family if they wanted or needed the convenience of their motor home, they might have been told it was not necessary. But they didn't ask; they just did it—and for that, we will always remember their warm kindness and hospitality. This was another example of God's grace *enabling* His people to share that which He had provided for them, another priceless blessing from God.

I had only been in the hospital a day or so when Daddy brought a uniformed man into my room; he was a highway patrol officer. The polite, middle-aged man asked a few questions regarding the wreck. I answered him with what were probably shallow, drug-induced responses, but the patrol officer was kind and sympathetic. He told us the people driving the two trucks who caused the wreck all knew one another. They had been celebrating the Fourth of July weekend by partying at a local bar and had left the bar under the influence of alcohol. The man driving the truck, who initiated the chain of events, was drunk and left the scene of the accident. He returned an hour later, after he had somewhat sobered up, and turned himself into the police.

Daddy was more enraged than I ever imagined possible. He was crying hysterically, and he told me, "We'll get that son of a bitch." Having never seen my daddy so angry, I remember being confused by his comment, and I told him the wreck had been an accident. I told him the guy didn't intentionally hit us. I am sure Daddy must have been somewhat puzzled by my reaction, as was everyone else, thinking my response was probably attributed to the drugs.

As any father would do, Daddy was attempting to assure his little girl he would protect her and see to it this man received the punishment he deserved for the pain and loss he had caused. Yet I had responded by not showing any hostility toward the man. My response was sincere; I felt no hatred toward him. I truly believed that what had happened had been a human mistake, an accident. In my troubled yet peaceful mind, I could not fathom anyone purposely causing this much pain and suffering on another human being.

Daddy expressed his rage to the patrol officer regarding the injuries I had received due to my wearing a seat belt. Others reminded Daddy that had I not been wearing the belt, I probably would not have lived through the wreck. The patrol officer went on to tell us he had responded to hundreds of wrecks in his career, and he had never seen one so horrendous with anyone pulled out alive. He told me it was a miracle I was alive. My seat belt, even though it caused me severe abdominal injury, was probably the only thing that had saved my life. I am certain he had not taken into consideration that I was still alive only because of the grace of God.

CHAPTER 3

In the Arms of an Angel

Jesus took the children in His arms and
placed His hands on their heads and blessed them.
—Mark 10:16

I gave my brother the name of the church my family and I had occasionally attended for the last two years and informed him the pastor there would probably be the one to perform the funeral. My brother contacted the pastor, but he declined, indicating he did not know us well enough to perform the service. I was appalled he had refused, but later I discovered I had indeed been blessed to have him decline. God showed us there was someone much more suited for the assignment of laying my family to rest.

My brother suggested the new pastor at the church I had attended throughout my youth, which was where he attended with his young family, and Mother and Daddy. I believe the pastor had met my family only once before when we attended church with my parents, but he did not personally know Larry, my children, or me. It turned out he was the gift from God. The pastor was young, and I later learned he had never performed a funeral before presented with this challenge. But, as in Acts 1:8, "he received the power as the Holy Spirit came upon him," and he demonstrated the power by showing our family love and consideration during our time of need.

The pastor drove to my hospital room some two hours away and asked if he could speak with me about Larry and the kids. He began by asking how Larry and I had met. I said Larry and I had been high school sweethearts, and after Larry had left Texas to attend an out-of-state college, we felt we did not want to be separated any longer so we married. We were both nineteen.

My mind immediately drifted away, and I began reminiscing about how Larry and I had actually become sweethearts; however, the words remained in my innermost, unspoken thoughts at that time. During our high school years, Larry was known throughout our community as being an outstanding athlete. I had a few dates with Larry's best friend, the quarterback of our football team, before I discovered Larry actually wanted a date with me. Larry, being the charmer he was, convinced me to bet him a kiss that he could make four touchdowns that week during the Friday night football game.

Even though I really had no desire to date Larry, I made the bet with him. After all, it was just a kiss, and we were gaining lots of attention from our friends, which if I remember correctly, was very important at the time! So being the normal, oblivious high school girl that I was, I bet him, not believing he could make four touchdowns and not knowing we were playing the weakest team in our district. Larry won the bet, making not four, but five touchdowns that night, many of which were the result of plays called by the quarterback I had wanted to date in the first place. Now that I think about it, I wonder if they were together on that plan. I'll never know, nor do I care because I was the true winner that night. I had received another gift from God. God knew the plans He had for me, and a few years later, I married a very loving man who became a great father to our children.

Pastor questioned me about Larry's coaching career, and I told him Larry would have been beginning his second year as the athletic director and football coach in the small town where we lived, his dream job. I told him Larry was a very good coach and teacher, and that he had, in fact, become a father figure to many of his students. He recognized the importance of scholastic and athletic training. Again, I laid there silently remembering Larry's personality as a coach; he was very strict but always remained kindhearted. He made men out of many of the boys and helped them develop their character in life. I recalled Larry removing a star player from his team because the boy had broken the team's no smoking rule. The boy's parents were, of course, irate, and made an effort to have Larry fired. Larry did not back down, informing the school administration and the boy's parents there would be no way to successfully teach discipline to the other teammates if he allowed the boy to play after the boy had blatantly broken the rules. Larry kept his job, the parents and administration backed down, the team lost their game, and he never regretted one action he made. I remember being so proud of him—a little nervous he would lose his much-needed job, but very proud!

I was unable to tell the pastor a great deal about my two children. I managed to give him the facts: birthdays, color of hair and eyes, and physical characteristics. But how can a mother express to someone how she really feels about her wonderful children and talk about how important they are in her life. In Mark 10:16, the disciples scolded some parents for bringing their children to Jesus and bothering him. The Bible says, "Jesus took the children in his arms and placed his hands on their heads and blessed them." This is a verse I hold close and take comfort in after losing my two precious children. I have the comforting satisfaction of knowing they are with God. He has placed His hands on their heads and blessed them with eternal life in heaven. I thank Him for this gift and praise Him daily for the assurance of knowing my beautiful, innocent children are cradled in His loving arms at this very moment!

CHAPTER 4

The End of Our Beginning

And though you started with little,
you will end with much.
—Job 8:7

The day of the funeral arrived. I remained in ICU, apparent it would not be possible for me to attend. Thankfully, my mother, my daddy, and one of my aunts chose to remain with me at the hospital during that time. Even though I wasn't sitting in the church, I was very much there in spirit. As I lay in the bed with my eyes closed, I could imagine the familiar church and the faces of those who would be attending. I never anticipated, however, that the small church literally overflowed with hundreds of family and friends who came to pay their respects and mourn the loss of my family. I knew the songs that were being sung, and I knew the kind and color of flowers that adorned Larry's casket and the two smaller ones positioned on each side of him.

A friend of mine recorded a local television station newscast of the funeral. The video beautifully captured the poignant scene of the young men of Larry's football team. They proudly wore their orange and white football jerseys and marched ceremoniously, yet tearfully, carrying the caskets to the three white hearses waiting in front of the small church on the hot July day. I believe many of those boys became men that day, as they learned at their tender age how it feels to lose not only their coach, but also a very good friend.

David thoughtfully arranged to record the funeral that allowed me to watch it later. Many weeks afterward, I sat on my parent's sofa in their living room with my mother and daddy on each side of me, our hands locked securely together. We wept as we heard the pastor talk about my family and explained why I was unable to attend the funeral. He did an outstanding job revealing my family's life.

Pastor had made the extra time and effort required to travel more than an hour to our home to visit with neighbors, school administrators, teachers, friends, and students to familiarize and discover every aspect of the lives that no longer existed. Pastor's attention to detail and the added effort he made to prepare for his first funeral showed brilliantly throughout the service.

Pastor described Larry's football program and his team, which scarcely had enough players, and who had not won a game during their last season. He described the desire Larry inspired in the young boys' hearts, teaching them the sport was not about how many games they won, but the personal integrity in which they played. He conveyed stories of football practices when Larry would have our young son, Cliff, stand in a spot among the much larger high school boys so they would have enough players to practice as a full team. The pastor beautifully painted a picture of Adrianne playing on the sidelines in her little dress, twirling her baton, and running water bottles out to the team when her daddy called for them.

All the familiar scenes the pastor so vividly described brought to my memory a note Larry once received from a woman in our town whom we didn't even know. In the note, she expressed her admiration of Larry's teaching efforts. She thanked him for the dignity and thoughtfulness his football team displayed as he instructed them to stop practice, remove their helmets, and stand at attention to pay their respect as her husband's funeral possession passed the practice field. This graciously written note vividly portrayed the character of the man with whom I had fallen in love many years before.

Pastor referenced King Solomon's observations concerning his own life throughout the book of Ecclesiastes. This reference proved to be an entirely accurate description of the life Larry and I had experienced together.

> The fastest runner doesn't always win the race,
> and the strongest warrior doesn't always win the battle.
> The wise sometimes go hungry,
> and the skillful are not necessarily wealthy.
> And those who are educated don't always lead
> successful lives.
> It is all decided by chance, by being in the right place
> at the right time.
> People can never predict when hard times might come.
> Like fish in a net or birds in a trap,
> people are caught by sudden tragedy.
> —Ecclesiastes 9:11–12

Larry and I labored diligently throughout our young married lives, yet we were never able to get ahead financially or in our careers. Only now do I understand what King Solomon meant throughout Ecclesiastes. Near the end of the king's life, he looked back on everything he had accomplished and the things he had gained. Only then did he understand that his achievements would not bring him happiness or wealth. Similarly, in our lives, I feel much of what Larry and I sought after was meaningless in God's overall purpose of life. We were successful, not in or of this world, but in the eyes of God. The world we live in is finite and unfair, and I do not believe it is at all what God intended it to be for us. God did not make this world to provide the rewards for which He wants us to strive. We will only receive those rewards in heaven.

In our lives, as in many lives today, it unfortunately takes the harsh reality of death before accomplishments are recognized. Our love and respect for each other as husband and wife, the integrity Larry strived to instill in his students, and the way in which we raised our children, were our only rewards in this world. Through God's grace, we possessed enough spiritual knowledge to build our life's foundation on our faith and trust in Him. As Larry sits this day in the presence of God Almighty, I believe he is currently reaping the rewards for which he worked so diligently throughout his short life. I pray someday I will join him, and we may rejoice in these rewards together.

I naturally wanted to attend my family's funeral, but I knew God kept me in the hospital for my own protection. I feared I would never have the closure I would receive from a funeral—the final, tearful good-bye, the last touch, or one last look at their faces. I sensed that being unable to attend was an instance when God knew what was best, and He sheltered me from the intense pain I would have endured by attending. Once again, I felt God's presence with me that day, and His compassion released me from the fears of death and the traditional ceremonies we perceive necessary today. I found comfort and peace in knowing my family was together experiencing the joy of being with our Father.

Larry and I were high school sweethearts, young married college students struggling to make ends meet, and beginning a family with only the faith of God in our pockets. It seemed we were just beginning our life together, and then there was this sudden, tragic end, "the end of our beginning."

CHAPTER 5

Responsibility for Our Decisions

Give me understanding and I will obey your
instructions,
I will put them into practice with all my heart.
—*Psalm 119:32*

The previous discussion with the highway patrol officer began me thinking about the sequence of events that led to me being in the hospital. What had happened? I lay alone in my bed and began putting events of the recent week together in my mind.

The four of us spent the week with my two aunts, cousins, and various other family and friends camping at a lake in southeastern Oklahoma. Larry and I had recently managed to scrape together enough money to purchase a used tent camper. We were going on our first family, weeklong vacation at last.

We purchased our camper from an ad in the newspaper, and when we picked it up, I remember the older couple telling Larry and me they certainly hoped we would enjoy it as much as they had while their children were young. Their kids were older now, and they didn't much care about camping with Mom and Dad anymore. We assured them we would continue to carry out their tradition with our own family. We explained we had camped in a tent up until this point, and we were looking forward to the luxury of the upgraded accommodations. I remember feeling a little melancholy for them since they were letting go of their past and fond memories with their children. Ironically, now all I have left are the memories from the week of camping with my husband and children.

We spent days planning and packing for the trip. Larry rebelliously changed out of his everyday football coach clothing for once and put on a brightly colored shirt I had purchased for him. We traveled the two hours to the state park, and as we were entering the area, a tire blew out on our camper trailer. Larry and I managed to change the small tire in the intense heat, and then we climbed back into our truck with sweat dripping off both of us. We cranked up the air conditioner as high as it would go and with a little disparagement in our voices said that this was some way to start our vacation! Little did we know what the week would have in store for us.

As our weeklong campout drew to an end, Larry and I decided it would be better to leave the campground on Saturday, July 5, rather than fight the heavier traffic, which would normally be on the Sunday following a three-day holiday weekend. We discussed the route we would take and off we went, sadly leaving the campgrounds we had enjoyed so much during the week.

We were driving west on a long straight stretch of a rural, two-lane highway. My daughter asked me if she could remove her seat belt so she could lie down to take a nap in the backseat. My son, with his sunburned, freckled face, then removed his seat belt and sat on the edge of the backseat, leaning between the two front bucket seats where my husband was driving and I was riding. The three of us talked about all the fun we experienced during our first true vacation and enthusiastically tried to decide where we could go the next time we had an opportunity to camp.

I remember looking down the narrow road as we continued discussing our plans. I noticed two eastbound pickup trucks closely following each other and heading directly toward us. Repeatedly, the rear truck kept pulling out into our westbound lane as if it was trying to pass the front one; however, each time it would fall back behind the other. The front truck seemed to speed up each time, not allowing the other to pass. I nervously told my husband to watch out for the trucks because they seemed to be playing with each other, to which he commented he had been watching them as well. I saw the back truck suddenly speed up and veer toward the outer edge of the road, as if trying to pass the other on the narrow shoulder.

The rear truck struck the passenger side rear bumper of the front truck forcing the front truck to cross the centerline into our westbound lane. This whole sequence of events lasted only a few seconds, but I knew instantaneously that we were going to be struck. I screamed, "They're going to hit us!" In that split second, my life as I knew it, changed forever. It happened so fast, Larry did not have time to apply the brakes. I felt the tremendous impact of vehicles colliding at full speed. Our vehicle came to rest upside down, and according to witnesses, it was so badly destroyed it was impossible to identify the make or model. Our small camper trailer was thrown from the truck hitch and tossed about like a plastic toy in the wind. Demolished, all its contents scattered along the road and side ditch.

In 1986, wearing a seat belt was more of a suggestion than an observed law. There had been reports it could help save lives in the case of an accident. Typically, my family wore our belts when traveling. Larry and I were wearing our belts; however, the driver's side door received the brunt of the direct impact killing Larry instantly.

My children had been wearing seat belts as well, but I had given permission to remove them. Cliff was pronounced dead at the scene that resulted from massive head and body trauma. From various reports, I learned Adrianne had been thrown from the vehicle, and when first responders arrived on the scene, they believed she had a weak pulse and tried desperately to save her young life. She was also pronounced dead despite the attempted heroics of the first responders. I have lived for years with the unsettling question, "If I had made Cliff and Adrianne wear their seat belts, would it have made a difference? Would they have lived?" Thankfully, God's mercy prevents me from ever knowing the answer to these questions, and I have come to believe knowing would serve no useful purpose whatsoever.

Most of the vehicles in that era were built with only a belt that fit across the lap, just below the waist. There were no shoulder straps to protect the upper body, as there are today, or do I remember if there was even such a thing as an air bag. The powerful impact of the vehicles forced the base of the bucket seat in which I was strapped, to tear away from the truck's heavy metal frame. As designed, my lap belt remained bolted to the truck's frame and restrained me from being thrown from the vehicle. My seat was ripped from its base, and it lay on its side almost completely inverted. This was the position I found myself when I awoke in the wreck. The tightness and pain I felt around my lower abdomen was my lap belt holding me securely in the truck.

The highway patrol officer who questioned me earlier in the hospital told me he had never seen anyone pulled out alive after such a violent crash. So why was I still alive? Why had God spared me but not my precious family? Why had we been in that exact spot on the highway when the trucks collided? If only we had not stopped earlier to buy soft drinks. Why hadn't we taken the different route as we had planned? Why didn't we travel home on a different day?

So many *ifs*! I began to wonder if I had done something in my life to deserve this. Was I being punished? I didn't think so, but maybe I should have been a better wife to Larry, or even a better mother to my children; I should have protected them better. As a child, my parents taught me to attend church every single week. Maybe Larry and I should have been more diligent in attending church regularly. Would that have changed the results of our situation?

One after another the questions kept coming. I knew in my soul that my husband, children, and I were just innocent bystanders. I believed we were blameless of doing anything to receive the punishment of this magnitude. The people driving the trucks made the decisions, which resulted in our wreck. My family made no bad decisions that day; we were simply at the wrong place at the wrong time. The only excellent choice made on that day was the moment I cried out for God's help. This is the definitive choice any of us can make in any circumstance to ask for His ultimate saving grace. I praise God for answering my prayer that day and allowing me in that instant to make the decision to follow Him.

CHAPTER 6

The Tapestry of Our Lives

For we are God's masterpiece.
He has created us anew in Christ Jesus,
so we can do the good things he planned for us long ago.
—Ephesians 2:10

Life is a hodgepodge of decisions we make every second of every day of our life. Thornton Wilder wrote a novel, *The Eighth Day*, about a man whose life is destroyed by bad luck. He and his family suffer, although they are innocent. At the end of the novel, there is no happy conclusion. Instead, Wilder reveals an image of a beautiful tapestry, which he explains represents our life. On the backside of the tapestry, the side of us our God sees, there is an assortment of threads weaving across one another in different lengths and different colors. Some of the threads have knots, some are unraveling, and some are securely tied. As we turn the tapestry over, we see it represents one of God's original designs, the design into which He has made us. In essence, we see ourselves, His masterpiece.

Sometimes, threads have to be stretched to their limit to reach their place on the tapestry, stretched even to the point of breaking. That was where I found myself. All I could see was the back of the tapestry. I was a stretched and broken thread. The question tore at my heart. Why would God pull me to the point of breaking?

I felt uncertainty. Had this happened because of something I had or had not done? All my life I had been taught how our God was a perfect God. He would protect us and keep us from harm if only we believed and trusted in Him. So when bad things happen to us, does it mean God is disciplining or punishing us for our actions? Did this mean I really didn't believe and trust in Him as I should?

I knew when God sent His only Son to die on the cross for our sins, He took away the need to ever punish or discipline us. At this very moment, I was beginning to question that belief. I knew, I even believed, God would not make us feel guilty about something that happens, such as not making my children wear their seat belts. Satan is the one who wants to make us feel guilty, to destroy us, not God.

God, our Father, does not want or allow anything bad to happen to us. Why? Because He loves us! We are His children, right? I did not want anything bad to happen to my children, and my earthly father did not want anything bad to happen to me either. Children should be able to trust that their father will protect them from all evil. But our earthly fathers cannot provide us that benefit. At some point in our lives, in maturity, we have the opportunity to make our own decisions, but that opportunity does not stop our fathers' desire for our safety. Then why did this happen? Had I not lived up to God's expectations as a Christian? Didn't God love me as only my heavenly Father could? Why hadn't He protected my family and me?

Of course, God wanted to protect me. I knew that, but it was difficult to understand as I continued to suffer. I John 5:4 states, "Every child of God defeats this evil world, and we achieve this victory through our faith." I knew I had faith, but did I have enough? I needed to hear from God what He was planning to do now that something really bad had happened to me. I felt my life was in such disarray. I realized God had already given me the answer to all the questions I had been asking. He demonstrated His answers by giving me His perfect peace; the peace I immediately felt upon calling out to Him, "the peace of God, which surpasses all understanding." I had no choice but to allow God to take care of me.

Now, if only I would allow God to do so and turn loose of the decisions I wanted to make for myself in my life. I would never hear actual words from God, but I would feel the same love that we are blessed to feel in a marriage or as a parent, that unspoken love and the look in the eyes that tells us what a person is feeling. As a child, I knew whether my mother approved or disapproved of my actions by looking at the expression on her face. I wanted, I needed, I had to have strength I currently did not have available to me as a human living in the flesh. God cannot live in a shallow heart; our heart is only as great as the love we allow God to place in it. So I would have to grow my heart to allow Him all the room He wanted because I needed Him more than anyone could imagine!

There's an old cliché I believe relates to how we can grow our hearts. It says, "Any fool can count the seeds in an apple, but only God knows how many apples are in a seed." Read that again. Now think about it for a minute; this clearly explains the message of our faith. Everything begins as a seed, and that seed has to be planted in order for it to grow. We cannot restrict or carry God's seed of faith around in our pockets and expect Him to grow there. We should never ask God if we should plant the seed, for this is why He has planted us here on earth, to grow our hearts. What does a seed represent in the cliché? It can be the seed of love, energy, wisdom, food, or generosity; anything we give to others is a seed we plant. This book is a seed I am planting. Planting is an act of faith. Plant an apple seed, a tree grows, and it produces many apples. In everything we do, we are acting in faith. Trusting the apples would grow, be picked, and many would be fed.

As in life, the number of seeds we plant increases the infinite number of hearts we can assist in growing. God wants us to plant these seeds continually and trust Him to do what man alone cannot. He expects us to never tire of planting and enjoying the harvests He will provide to us. We must keep in mind that we can't change what has already been planted—our pasts. We can't plant an apple seed and pray for corn. It won't happen. If we want corn, we have to plant corn. In this regard, we live with what we have planted, so be happy, don't give up, don't tire of planting other seeds, a harvest of blessings await you.

Jesus tells us, "Anyone with ears to hear should listen and understand." He is not referring to the kind of hearing we use when we listen to music. Jesus wants us to hear and apply His Word to our everyday lives, and use them in our decision-making process. In order for us to understand what Jesus is saying, we must first believe and trust the Word. Jesus was saying to me, "I am your Lord, let me live in your heart in love, and you will feel the wonderful peace I have to offer to you." I knew in order to feel this peace God promises, I would have to spend time with Him, listening, planting, growing, and harvesting His instructions. I would have to become fertile soil to grow His Word.

Friends and family members offered many thoughts and insights in an attempt to help me understand what had happened. Their intentions were sincere, loving, and caring, but the words and assurances they offered did not heal the pain or help me understand. "Be thankful God has taken your sinless children out of this evil world." "They are in a better place now." "God needed a good coach." "The people who caused this wreck will be punished." "God doesn't give us more than we can bear." I heard them all, but few offered any comfort to my injured soul.

My faith assured and guaranteed me God had not given me more than I could bear. He did not cause this bad thing to happen to me. Instead, He gave me the assurance to know that if I followed Him in my faith, He would stay with me, guide me, and love me forever. When I cried out in pain for God to help me on that hot July afternoon, He took over every aspect of my life and began to grow in my heart. God loved me; that was the only thing that would help me survive. He hadn't lost a child as I had; He sacrificed His son for our sins. Who better to understand the pain and loss I felt!

The sacrifice of God's son, Jesus, is one that I cannot begin to comprehend as a mother. I lost my children, by no choice of my own, and I know the pain I experienced. Try to imagine the pain God must have endured as He allowed his only son to die an unspeakable death on the cross for our sins! As an earthly mother, what must Mary have gone through as she watched her son die on the cross, knowing God had made such a sacrificial decision for the sinful people living among her.

In Genesis 22:2, imagine what Abraham must have felt as God called to him and said, "Take your son, your only son—yes, Isaac, who you love so much—and go to the land of Moriah. Go and sacrifice him as a burnt offering on one of the mountains, which I will show you." Picture the troubled Abraham as he followed God's instructions. Then imagine the sense of relief he must have felt as he picked up his knife to kill his only son and heard the angel say, "Do not to hurt him in any way, for now I know that you truly fear God" (Genesis 22:12). I'm not sure what emotions I would have felt had I been in Abraham's place—relief, anger, or gladness. That, my friends, is the ultimate in faith, trust, love, and peace. I wanted to have that kind of faith. I needed that kind of peace!

CHAPTER 7

Healing is More Than the Absence of Pain

I am not alone because my Father is with me.
I have told you all this so that you may be in peace.
Here on earth you will have many trials and sorrows.
But take heart, because I have overcome this world.
—John 16:31b; 32–33

A s Jesus prepared himself to die on the cross for our sins, He explained to His disciples to take courage, they would not be alone. It takes an abundance of faith to believe we are not alone in a world that is so disharmonious with Christ. We must have faith throughout our weakness. Jesus had not abandoned me in my struggles, in fact, just the opposite. He had presented me with the ultimate victory of peace.

My parents decided to transfer me to a hospital closer to their home. As I was secured in the ambulance, my brother, Danny, insisted on riding in the back with me. When he heard me groan in pain, I heard him complain to the driver to take it easy. He told the driver his little sister was hurting. Oh, those endearing words, "little sister." I guess I will always be a little sister to both my brothers, and I would have it no other way, since they will always be my big brothers whom I admire.

Danny would tell me where we were along the way, landmarks I would know to help me recognize where we were along the drive as I lay on the gurney in the ambulance. He told me when we were heading south through our childhood hometown. I knew exactly where we were. I visualized my friend's home just off the highway, and the home where I had spent my teenage years and where my parents still lived. Danny asked me if I was hurting because he noticed tears flowing down my cheeks. I told him I knew we had just passed the cemetery on the north end of town where my family had been laid to rest a few days before. He reached down and gently wiped away my tears.

Once I arrived in the new location, I was moved to a very nice private room. It wasn't like any hospital room I had seen before. It was similar to a bedroom, only it contained a hospital bed. I remember thinking this was probably the kind of room reserved for dignitaries. I thought, *"Why would they place me in a room like this?"* I recognize now that I was being protected from grasping the magnitude of events that had transpired in my life. I had never been one to desire attention, and no place in my mind had I ever believed I deserved anything special. The unique treatment I was receiving seemed so unnecessary to me. The realization of how my life had changed was incomprehensible; I knew what had happened, and I remained in God's glorious peace.

The new nurses and doctors were very attentive to me as I began my physical and emotional healing process. The doctors restricted my visitors to enable me time to rest and begin recovery. Quickly, the number of guests seemed to dwindle to an occasional visitor. The lives around me were continuing, and it appeared that what had happened to their friends was slowly becoming a passing memory. Compassion and mourning is a passing thing for most. They care, but not enough to make a real change in their lives to help. One day, as I realized people around me were moving on with their everyday lives, I found myself more and more alone. My parents and other family members were there for me, but even they had their own lives to live, and I understood this. I did not expect or want them with me every minute of every day.

Strength eventually began returning to my weak body, and soon I could get out of bed alone. My body was slowly improving as I worked in rehab to heal my physical wounds. The physical pain within my body was becoming tolerable. The emergency room doctors saved my life with an operation that pieced together the severed muscles across my lower abdomen. The lacerations on my face were beginning to heal, even though occasionally another piece of glass would work its way to the surface from between the stitches.

The natural reflex during a collision is to raise your arms to protect yourself, which is exactly what I had done. I had raised my left arm to the dash, and the force of the impact fractured my elbow resulting in severe nerve damage. The injury left no feeling in my arm from the elbow down, and my hand hung limp from my wrist. I could lift my arm, but there was no feeling in my wrist or fingers. A few days after arriving at the local hospital, doctors performed surgery. They placed a pin in my elbow to ensure my arm healed properly. My arm was placed in a hard plastic brace from my elbow to my fingertips to prevent the muscles from compensating and adjusting to the limpness of my wrist. I began physical therapy, and the doctors assured me that within eight to ten weeks I would regain feeling in my fingers.

A dear friend of our family came to visit me one day. We spoke for a short time, and then with tears in his eyes, he handed me an envelope. In it was a new bank account checkbook. In a column titled Balance was a dollar amount. He told me many people cared and in an effort to help, they decided to open an account for me. He continued to tell me that people would be depositing money in it for my use. I laid there in shock. How could people be so kind, and what had I done to deserve this! I knew people made this type of "love offering" all the time, I had even given at times, but I couldn't believe they were doing it for me.

For quite some time, I received deposit slips from the bank informing me of contributions that had been made into this account, and each time I opened the envelopes, tears would fill my eyes. I knew I needed the money; Larry and I did not have a savings account, but I had never expected this kind of generosity from so many kind people, even from people who didn't know me.

The national news had covered the story of the wreck. I received cards, notes, and letters from all over the country. I remember one card in particular from out of state that had a five-dollar bill inside it. In spotty ink and poor, unsteady penmanship was printed, "May God be with you."

Someone once said anyone could be kind. Kindness is a ministry achieved by all men, rich and poor, learned and illiterate. That is the only note I remember receiving, and it could not have touched me anymore had it been filled with five thousand dollars. This taught me a valuable lesson; it doesn't matter how much we give, what really matters is the heart with which we give it. I certainly came to know many people who had huge hearts during this time.

The next several quiet weeks allowed me time alone to begin thinking about the reality of the life in which I had been placed. I had so many questions, so many serious decisions to make about my future, something I had never faced before. I had graduated from high school and attended a local college while living at home with my parents. One year later, I married my high school sweetheart, and we moved away to an out of state college town to create our new lives together. In my entire life, I had never been alone or lived by myself. Even with all the health issues, questions, and decisions looming, I was never fearful of the life I had to face. I remained in a sense of peace, a peace I had never known before. What was this feeling within me? Don't misunderstand. I felt the tremendous sorrow in my heart, the incredible sense of loss, but there was an incredible feeling in me that calmed my inner self, something I did not have control over.

After several more weeks in the hospital, I was released to stay with my parents. They were the only constant in my life at this point. They accepted me back into their home as if I had never left thirteen years before. Complications from my initial injuries continued to plague my already damaged body. I underwent several more surgeries in the upcoming months, and my parents continued to care for me in every respect.

Parents never lose the caring response for their children, and mine were there to console me at every turn. I'm not sure what I would have done if they had not been there for me. In fact, I believe they were more worried about my future than I was; they had not felt the peace with which God had blessed me. I did not fully understand at the time that God had already taken complete control of my life.

My mom and dad had again become parental figures. They must have spent sleepless nights worrying about my future. They assumed I would want to continue living with them even after my body had physically healed. I'm sure they thought there was no way I could continue on my own, and I didn't even know that for sure. My life as I knew it was over. My little-girl dream of marrying and having children had been fulfilled beginning thirteen years ago, and now it was over. I had decisions to make!

Larry's parents and I remained in touch, but we did not see one another very often. It was surely difficult for them, as it was for me. I was probably not there for them as much as I should have been, even though I believe it would have been somewhat bittersweet for them to be around me. They had experienced the very painful loss of a son and their only grandchildren.

Larry's dad, "Coach," as I always called him, had suffered a debilitating stroke several years before Larry's death, which forced him to retire from coaching, his lifelong love, and profession. Larry held a special bond with his dad. He consulted with his dad on many occasions and even had him give motivational speeches to his teams. I am sure Larry's death compounded a tremendous void in Coach's life. Larry's mother later told me Coach had a very difficult time trying to recover from the loss of his youngest son. He was somewhat confined to their home due to his health, and this complicated his opportunity for healing. Coach passed away a few years later from continued health issues, and I'm sure, a broken heart.

Larry's mom, Frances, had been in the school business for decades, and throughout her loss, she continued teaching and gaining support from colleagues and the children she taught. She had been a very young mother. She dropped out of high school, and at the age of fifteen, already had two sons ten months apart. Once the boys were older, she returned to continue her education and achieved a master's degree. She became a math teacher and taught for years while Coach continued his coaching career. I remember her telling me she knew it was time to retire when she began teaching the children of her first students. She became a grandmother at thirty-eight and loved having the time to spend and play with her two grandchildren; something I am sure she did not have when she had her two little boys. I always admired her for never giving up on the situations she faced in her life. She endured with a goal in mind, helped support her family, and all the while kept alive her dream of teaching.

Larry's brother was only ten months older than Larry was. The two boys practically grew up as twins. The loss of his brother was devastating for him. He had also followed his father's example and become a high school coach right after college. I don't know why, but he left his coaching career shortly after the death of Larry and his father. I'm sure it must have been just too painful to continue a life in the coaching world without his two comrades. He is now self-employed and helps his mother operate the family farm and livestock.

The one thing Larry's family can rest assured in is that they will always remain an important part of my life. They were always there for us throughout our lives. They were wonderful parents to their two sons and awesome grandparents to our two children. They helped support Larry and I while he was in college and struggling financially with a new baby. I had been laid off from my job, and Larry felt he needed to quit college to support his new young family. Through their own experiences, his parents knew the importance of a higher education, and they helped us in every way possible to keep Larry in college until he graduated. I will always be grateful to them and will forever love and cherish the memories I have of our time together.

I continued living with my parents for several more weeks. Guests continued to come visit me, people I hadn't seen in years. It was healing in a sort of way, but sad in another. Many of the visiting friends had been part of our married life. The Bible tells us when a man and woman marry the two become one. When a spouse is gone, through death or even divorce, it feels as if the one remaining becomes only half of what once was. This was what I felt being around these friends, only half of a friendship. There was something missing. Larry was gone. During one visit with old friends, I suddenly realized things were never going to be the same. In losing Larry, I lost many of our friends. It was not something that consciously happened; it was just something that occurred in the natural flow of life.

There was much business to take care of while I continued to recover at my parents' home. Larry and I did not have a will; something I recognize now as being very important, regardless of age. The younger we are, the more difficult it is to discuss dying; we all feel invincible at a young age. However, let me suggest at the very least, put in your own words or let someone close to you know your desires. Larry and I had never discussed our deaths—where we wanted to be buried, the dispersal of our property, or most importantly, the custody of our children.

I faced the frightening thought of what would have happened to our children had they survived and Larry and I had been killed. Who would have cared for them? I certainly appreciate now how important it is to make your decisions known. However, it was too late for Larry and me. I had to make all the decisions by myself now, and I struggled with the answers to those questions, not knowing how Larry and I would have handled these things together. I felt so alone making decisions. After the loss of a loved one, it is a terrible time to have to make choices. Make them together, and before it is too late.

The company I worked for in Wichita Falls had been very understanding throughout my recovery. I had worked for them only one year and had taken a week off to go on our vacation. I had health insurance through the company, and according to the human resources director, I had done something very unusual for an employee my age. I had checked a box, which allowed the company to take a small monthly deduction for accidental death insurance on my husband and myself. I didn't even remember doing it, but when the director came to my parents' house, he was delighted to inform me of my choice. The insurance check would offer me some time to make decisions relative to the next steps in my life.

The human resources director and my boss assured me I would have a job when or if I ever decided to return to work. I didn't know how long my physical healing would take or if I would have the emotional strength to return. It had been several weeks and I still had no feeling in my wrist or fingers, and my arm remained in a brace. How could I return to secretarial work with just one hand? Regardless of my concern, they assured me I could take as long as I needed to decide. It was comforting to know I still had a job.

I look back now and know I could have given up at this point, probably gone on disability, taken the path of least resistance, but I never even considered such a thing. I could not explain it, but the peace I received immediately following the wreck had consistently remained within me, and I recognized an inner drive to heal and go on with my life.

My boss, Bob, came to my parents' house several times to have me take care of additional insurance paperwork, or deliver cards from coworkers, or sometimes simply to visit. I was beginning to feel restless in the house and ready to get out. I had only known Bob and his wife for a little more than a year, and I always felt Bob had a very dry sense of humor. I thought he was a little arrogant, but soon realized he was a very tenderhearted man. He was willing to sit, talk, and listen to me for long periods. Occasionally, he would visit and ask me if I wanted to go for a ride to the company's Gainesville subsidiary office. It was nice to just get out of the house and talk to each other about work and not about what had happened to me.

Once I remember Bob and I were returning to my home, and as we passed through Gainesville, I asked him if we could drive through the small wooded city park located just off the highway. It was a beautiful early autumn day, and the leaves were beginning to change. He stopped the car, and we decided to walk through the leaves that had begun to fall. When I stepped out of his car, I sensed a familiar, upsetting odor. I could smell the heat from the engine, and it immediately took me back to the crash. It was the first time I had broken down in front of Bob, actually in front of anyone. We sat across from one another at a picnic table under the falling leaves, and there I told him about my memories of the wreck.

Bob was really the first one I had ever told about the accident. He was exactly what I needed—a friend willing to listen and someone I could talk to about my future. Since he was outside my family support group, I thought he could possibly see things from a different perspective. I wasn't afraid of upsetting him with my concerns. He was a kind, caring man, and even though he was my boss, I felt extremely comfortable talking to him about my future.

CHAPTER 8

Facing the Giants

*So David triumphed over the Philistine giant
with only a sling and a stone, for he had no sword.*
—*1 Samuel 17:50*

Raised in a Christian home, God had always been an integral part of my life. Daddy was an adult Sunday school teacher for more than fifty years. He was also a substitute preacher in the local area churches. Mother was very active as well and helped organize and lead the youth fellowship in our church for several years. She was also involved in the women's ministries. As a young girl, I spent every week in Sunday school and church, and I gave my life to Christ at the age of fifteen. I knew who God was, but I did not know Him on an experiential level. At thirty-two, I found I was still an immature Christian. I did not know how to trust and live in Jesus Christ.

As the days of emotional and physical healing continued in my life, I felt the power of God more and more. The sensation of peace I felt during the past few months was God Himself living in and caring for me. He removed the panic most people feel if they were in my situation. God told the crippled man to "pick up his mat and walk," and I knew He was telling me to "pick up my life and live." Whether God saved my life that day or He simply took over when I called out to Him while lying in the wreck, for whatever reason, I was alive, and I wanted to live in Him.

I prayed every day asking God to help me make the decisions I needed to make. Most of my friends lived in the area where I had worked, and a good job awaited me. After many prayers, I came to believe the familiar surroundings and the job was the logical place for me to continue my life.

Larry and I had purchased a new mobile home when we moved to Petrolia where he was the school's athletic director. I knew I could not go back to our house. I could not live there as if everything was the same. I had not returned to the house since we left on our camping trip almost three months before. Mother and Daddy took me to my house early one morning and in one day, we painfully went through every item.

When I opened the front door to the house and walked inside, I heard it, the silence I had heard during the wreck. I knew the house. I knew where the cold north wind would whistle in around a window. I remembered how every stain on the carpet had gotten there, and whose toys were still lying around the cluttered living room. What was unfamiliar to me was the silence. I remembered time and time again standing in the kitchen after a long day at work, the kids running in with their dirty little hands, and as they grabbed the refrigerator door, asked me what was for supper. I remembered it all. The memories washed over me like a powerful ocean wave crashing against the shoreline rocks. The house felt so empty, so lonesome. What once was our home was now all so strange to me.

After my parents and I pulled ourselves together emotionally, Daddy backed his big truck to the deck he had built for us just a few months before, and Mother began helping me make the difficult decisions. I began to separate the things I could not part with, the things I wanted to donate, and I disposed of the remainder. It was not easy, but it had to be done, and I certainly could not allow anyone to do this for me. Most items I picked up brought back a flood of memories, and the tears flowed like a river. The three of us worked tirelessly, and at the end of the day, we left the house with only a few boxes of memories. I had already made the decision to sell the house and the land where the house was located. With this sale, my connections with my family's physical past would be gone.

During the past years, I have gone through a few of the boxes and wondered why I decided to keep certain things. I knew some items were treasures only I would appreciate in years to come. I kept Larry's two high school track medals from 1972 when he won the Class A State Championship in the Shot Put and Discus. I kept the little white leather Bible my parents had given me when I joined the church and on which I carried my wedding bouquet as I walked down the aisle to marry Larry. Still in the Bible, a small, yellowed piece of paper with a handwritten note from my daddy simply stating, "I love you," which he had secretly placed inside the book on my wedding day.

Cliff and Adrianne's things were much different. Their lives had been so short, yet so joyful to me. I kept Cliff's baseball uniform from his first and only season of Little League, which he had just completed before our vacation. I removed from his bedroom shelves the miniature green John Deere tractors Daddy had given his first grandson while he was still a baby. The guitar Cliff had received his last Christmas sat in the corner of his room where he had left it after his daddy had given him his final lesson.

I treasure Larry's guitar, and to this day, I can still close my eyes and see him sitting on the hearth singing in his soulful, Elvis-like tone. I still remember the photo I took several years ago of him singing to his toddler daughter, Adrianne. She was smiling from ear to ear and swaying her hips rhythmically back and forth while flinging her little arms up in the air dancing for her daddy.

I kept Adrianne's orange and white pompoms, which she carried to every one of her daddy's football games. I packed away one special doll of hers, a handmade Cabbage Patch named Annie, Adrianne's nickname. Adrianne had surprised Larry and me at the last minute by telling Santa she wanted one of the dolls for Christmas. The real ones were nowhere to be found in the stores that year, so late one night after work, I drove across Dallas to pick up a doll handmade to resemble Adrianne and dressed in a little dress similar to one her grandma had made for her. I also carefully packed away several of Adrianne's dresses that my mother and Larry's grandmother, her great-grandmother had hand stitched for her.

I removed framed photos from the walls, and as I removed Cliff's last school picture from the hallway, the one with the black eye, I felt tears swell, and a smile come to my face. I repeated the story to Mother and Daddy how he had gotten the black eye the day before school photos were to be taken. He and Adrianne had been fighting over something, and as he picked up the corded telephone to call me at work to tell on his sister, she grabbed the receiver, swung it at him, and hit him in the eye. That poor child took relentless teasing because his little sister had given him a black eye.

When I walked out of our home that day, I left behind memories that only I remembered. There were the everyday things, you know, the things that aren't important enough to tell anyone about, but will always remain a fond memory of mine. I suddenly recognized the immense void in my life. It was as if my heart was being ripped right out of my chest as I locked the door behind me that afternoon. I no longer had my spouse with whom to share my everyday happenings, and I was no longer the small town coach's wife. My motherly responsibilities were gone as well. There would be no more lunches to prepare, no more spelling words to call out, no more long hair to detangle, no faces or noses to wipe, no bandages to apply, no black eyes to ice—there was just me.

I came to the harsh realization that I was alone! I had my parents and other family members, but I was on my own, something I had never felt before. It was somewhat frightening, but I could feel a new emotion coming over me. Along with the peace I had felt all along, I felt surprisingly strong and fearless. I must have felt a little like David the king of Israel did when he faced the Philistine giant, Goliath. It has been said Goliath was more than nine feet tall, wore heavy armor, and carried a sword and a long spear. Nathaniel Hawthorne once said, "The past lies upon the present like a giant's dead body." My new world seemed like a giant to me at this moment, and I knew how small I felt living in it. However, when I pushed myself out from under the giant's weight and began to fight, I knew I was not alone spiritually. If we face impossible situations from God's point of view, we can put what we consider our giant problems into perspective. Once we clearly see what is ahead of us and are following His guidance, God is with us every step of the way. When we ask God for help, He is always waiting to give it, allowing us to gain the strength to face life's giants. I felt like shouting at the top of my lungs, "Let the games begin!"

CHAPTER 9

One Day at a Time

*Give all your worries to God,
for he cares about you.*
—1 Peter 5:7

My brother, David, repaired my old car so I would have reliable transportation to return to my job. The people I worked with at the small office were tremendously compassionate and caring. One of my coworkers and his wife owned a home not far from our office, and they had an upstairs garage apartment in their backyard. The couple offered the apartment to me, and before I knew it, everyone from the office was helping my parents move my few pieces of furniture and belongings into my new home. The apartment was tiny, but in it I felt safe knowing friends were only a few yards away. This was very comforting since I had never lived alone.

The doctors told me the nerve damage in my left arm would likely heal in eight to ten weeks, but I still had no feeling in my fingers when I returned to work part-time in mid-September. I performed my job duties as always, but instead of typing more than one hundred words a minute as I had previously done, I was now doing the right-handed hunt-

and-peck on the keyboard. One day as I sat at the only office computer, I began feeling my fingers tingling, and by the end of the day, I had regained most of the use of my hand and fingers. I wanted to jump for joy, but first of all, I praised God for his remarkable healing powers.

At first, every day seemed to drag on endlessly, and every day something would send me off into a flood of emotions. I never knew when the tears would begin. I tried at first to hide my emotions from the other employees, but since I worked at the front desk in the office, it was very difficult. On one of my first days back, my boss, Bob, saw me fighting back tears and asked me to come into his office. I walked in, probably looking pathetic with my red nose dripping and my eyes swollen to the point of barely being able to see. I wasn't sure why he wanted to speak to me. Fear overcame me. Was he tired of seeing me cry? Had my work been affected? I didn't know. I was anxious when I walked into his office, as he was my boss, not a sympathetic coworker. I walked in, he closed the door, and my heart leaped with panic. I sat across the desk from him in the very chair where I had interviewed just a year before, and he simply reached across and handed me a box of tissues.

My crying sessions went on for what seemed forever. There were so many different reasons for my tears. I didn't believe I felt sorry for myself, but in some ways, I'm sure I did. I cried mostly because I felt a tremendous sense of absence in my life. I missed my family terribly, even though I knew I had many friends and family surrounding me. I enjoyed being around my coworkers, but at the end of each day, they had loved ones to go home to at night. I had no one.

My crying became a daily ritual. As the tears began, Bob allowed me to sit quietly and sniffle in his office. Often we would not even speak a word to each other, and he would continue with his work. His office became a place of sanctuary for me. I would sit, tears flowing, and look out the window. I'm not sure how many boxes of tissues I went through those weeks, but I assure you, there were many. I would continue to apologize for my tears for fear Bob believed it was affecting my job; however, he continued to tell me not to worry about it. One day as I apologized once again, he remarked, "Just take it one day at a time." This old adage became my motto. I would not think or worry about tomorrow, but just try to get through one day at a time. In the book of Matthew, Jesus asks us, "Can all your worries add a single moment to your life? Don't worry about tomorrow, for tomorrow will bring its own worries. Today's trouble is enough for today." (Matthew 6:34) This is a wonderful scripture, and one I continue to live by today.

Some time later, as I was preparing to leave the office for the day, Bob, who was walking out the front door, turned and asked, "Did you realize you didn't cry today?" He was right, I hadn't. I hadn't cried for the entire day, but of course, the realization made me begin to cry. This time though they were tears of joy, a sign I was beginning to heal emotionally.

God expected me to plan for my future but not to worry about it. My faithfulness in His guidance would not allow my worries to affect my relationship with Him. On occasion, the tears would return, but more and more I realized the episodes were coming farther and farther apart. I knew there would never be a day when thinking of my family wouldn't cause a burning in my eyes and the tears to begin.

Throughout the book of Matthew, the apostle outlines reasons why we should not worry. These are words for all of us to live by, regardless of our circumstances.

- The same God who created life in you can be trusted with the details of your life.
- Worrying about the future hampers your efforts for today.
- Worrying is more harmful than helpful.
- God does not ignore those who depend on him.
- Worrying shows a lack of faith in and understanding of God.
- Worrying keeps us from challenges God wants us to pursue.

- Living one day at a time keeps us from being consumed with worry.

Jesus explains to us that worry can be sinful, it can damage your health, disrupt your productivity, and it will negatively affect the way we treat others. Most of all, worrying reduces our ability to trust in God, which should be reason enough not to do it. However, He does not expect us to be oblivious to the situations around us. He knows and expects us to be concerned because after all, we are human. There is a huge difference between worry and concern—worry immobilizes and concern moves us to action. Concern means to pray, plan, and act according to God's guidance.

So how could I face each day with worry when Jesus so plainly teaches us there are so many reasons not to do so. Worry is such a waste of time! If we will trust and have faith in Him, He tells us clearly that He will take care of us. I had to learn not to be consumed by fear and to trust God completely.

I have a dear friend who will acknowledge she is a bit controlling. She has always said she knew God heard her when she prayed, but she confesses she doesn't believe He wants her to sit around and wait for an answer. He probably needed her to help Him answer those prayers. I love that about her, and I love that she admits she struggles with this. As a result, all of her girlfriends have to help her by telling her to turn loose and let God take care of whatever she prayed about. She does, but not without a squinting twinkle in her eye, a smile, and one last, "Are you sure He doesn't need me to help Him?" During the last few years, she has matured in her faith in God, she has become more trusting as she has seen His works first hand, and she trusts Him more each day.

CHAPTER 10

Wings of Eagles

But those who trust in the Lord will find new strength.
They will soar high on wings like eagles.
They will run and not grow weary.
They will walk and not faint.
—Isaiah 40:31

At this time in my life, I needed strength, not physical but spiritual strength. In the book of Isaiah, the prophet tries to impart on us how God's power and strength will never diminish. We will always be able to call on Him as our source of strength, and He will never grow weary of helping us. We must trust in the Lord and have faith that He will fulfill His promises to us.

A few months after I returned to work, I received a call from a victim advocate relating to my upcoming trial. She explained the events that were to follow and tried to prepare me for the things I would hear and witness during the proceedings. She was very kind and seemed genuinely worried the trial would be unpleasant and difficult for me.

In my mind, I believed once the trial commenced, I could handle the situation; everything I had endured, this would seem like a piece of cake. I was certain the justice system would progress systematically, just like in the movies. The criminal who caused my loss would be tried, found guilty by a jury of his peers, sentenced, and imprisoned for a considerable amount of time—the end of the show. However, that piece of cake I imagined savoring spoiled very quickly!

During our conversation, the advocate informed me of the judge's recent decision to reduce the three counts of felony vehicular manslaughter to negligent homicide, a lesser misdemeanor charge. I questioned the change, which I knew would allow a much lighter sentence handed down by a jury. The defense attorney presented a motion to the judge during a preliminary hearing in which he proposed the accused had not been drinking prior to the wreck, but only drank after he had left the scene of the accident, and the judge granted this motion. The accident reports stated the defendant left the scene of the accident and was witnessed throwing beer cans out of his truck. He did not return to the scene for almost two hours. His blood alcohol level was finally tested, and it proved slightly below what the law defines as legally impaired.

I was bewildered. How could this be happening? Hadn't the judge understood the defendant left the scene allowing him time to sober up? Wouldn't this fact be taken into consideration? Apparently not! The advocate also warned me that I should not expect a severe prison term to be awarded. She was attempting to prepare me for the appalling ordeal I would soon face.

The advocate also said I should realize that unfortunately the wreck occurred in a small, rural area where drinking and driving was accepted. She informed me that there was a chance many of the prospective jurors would be compassionate toward the defendant because they either knew him, his family, or his buddies. I realized I was dealing with a good ole boy mindset, and the jurors would likely want to allow him another chance instead of severely punishing him.

Where was the system I had depended on to bring my family justice? I wanted this man held accountable for the actions he had taken on July 5, 1986. I felt there was no difference in his decision to drive while intoxicated and killing three people than if he had picked up a rifle and shot each of them. It was his decision, no one else's! My family was innocent victims that deserved justice.

My heart and soul were crushed after receiving this news. How could the justice system be so calloused toward my family's deaths? This was so wrong! In all probability, the system was not going to pass down a severe penalty to this man. He would be allowed to walk the streets as if nothing had happened. The advocate was compassionate toward my complaints, but she informed me there wasn't much I could do. I was taken aback when she told me that since I had moved on with my life it would further hinder the chance of a serious penalty. Was she serious? Why shouldn't I be allowed to continue living my life? The wreck happened more than a year before. She even recommended I not publicize how I was moving on with my life by returning to work and socializing. This was becoming too much for me to handle!

I questioned the advocate about how I could change these misconceptions that had surfaced. She informed me the only way I might change the potential outcome of this trial would be to petition the courts for a change of venue. This would at least take the proceedings out of the local judicial system, which could possibly increase the chance of a more serious judgment. The petition might force the courts to consider that the defendant left the scene of the accident before he was tested for alcohol, which in itself was a crime. The phone call ended, and I found myself trying not to take what I had heard personal, but I still felt defeated. I was mad! I wanted justice, and I had just learned that in all probability, I would have none.

I returned to my apartment at the end of the day and considered my options. The first thing that came to my mind was I needed to pray, pray fervently! I picked up my Bible and tried to find answers to why this was happening. Hadn't I been through enough? I knew God was with me, but how could I fight the entire judicial system? That's when I read and understood I was not alone. God was on my side. Paul tells us in Ephesians 6:10 to "put on every piece of God's armor, so that we may be able to stand against all strategies of Satan and evil." Okay, I was strong enough to stand up against this evil. But what kind of armor did I have to protect and help my family receive the justice they deserved?

Beginning early the next day, I began making phone calls and learned I would need to have the courts file for a change of venue. This would be my first course of action; however, when I spoke to an attorney, he informed me the judge would probably not see the need for a change of venue and would deny the motion. I told him this would not be satisfactory to me, the victim, if the trial were held in the small hometown of the accused. The attorney also told me that public pressure would possibly be the only way the trial would be moved. He suggested perhaps a letter from me would help, but he informed me it would be improper for me to address the judge directly.

No problem, I could gain public attention by writing a letter to the editor of the local newspaper, thus publically encouraging the judge to understand the need for this change. Then I remembered what I had read in the Bible the night before, "put on every piece of God's armor." I had armor, lots of armor in the form of church, family, and friends, I wrote another letter to my pieces of armor. I called upon God's army to help me fight this battle.

I mailed out more than one hundred letters to everyone I knew as well as to the local newspapers in the surrounding areas where the trial was to be held. I simply told everyone what was happening and that I needed their help. I enclosed a copy of a letter I had mailed to the governor of Oklahoma explaining this travesty. I never heard back from the governor himself, but received a letter from an aide stating the governor was sorry for my loss, but regretted he could not do anything to assist me. I was not giving up!

I appealed to everyone I knew, and I asked every person to write a letter respectfully requesting a fair and impartial trial. I felt I had done everything to make a difference. There was no way in my wildest imagination could I have known what would happen next. Shortly after I mailed my letters, I began receiving copies of letters from people to whom I had written. An Oklahoma newspaper called to inform me they were receiving numerous correspondence and told me there was no way they could publish all of them; however, every day for some time they printed several full pages of letters. They were kind enough to send me copies of the pages and any articles they published about the trial.

I had known I needed the assistance of supreme powers to make a difference in this trial, and I was satisfied the arrows of God's army were successful in striking their target. God's armor had protected me, and I had achieved my goal. The trial was moved! God had given me the power of his Holy Spirit and His armor in the form of relationships to fight this battle.

However, the feeling of satisfaction was short lived. The trial was moved to a another town less than one hour away. Jury selection was finally completed and the trial was set to begin. The wreck had happened more than a year before. It was finally time to make this nightmare a part of my past. My family and I arrived at the small downtown courthouse the morning of the trial only to learn more discouraging news.

The district attorney asked to meet my family and me in private prior to entering the courtroom. He proceeded to tell us the defendant wanted to plea bargain instead of going to trial. He would plead guilty to three counts of negligent homicide, a misdemeanor serving consecutive sentences of one year each for the three deaths he had caused. This meant he would serve one year, and then if the justice system felt it was necessary, he would serve another and then another.

My heart sank. Really? One year each was all Larry, Cliff, and Adrianne's lives were worth in the justice system? This had to be a bad dream! My first response was no way would I allow this disrespect to my family. The district attorney representing the state and my family suggested I accept the plea bargain. He said there was no way this man would ever receive his just punishment. God spoke to me, and in my heart, I knew he was telling me the truth, even if I didn't want to hear it.

I couldn't believe the words I spoke when I told the district attorney to accept the plea bargain. I emotionally broke down. I didn't want to experience the stress and anxiety of the trial any longer. It had now been well over a year since the loss of my family, and I was exhausted in fighting these emotions every day!

I saw the defendant that day as he entered the courtroom. He looked straight into my eyes and never blinked or said a word; he just stared at me as he walked by. As the court proceedings commenced, the judge asked the defendant to stand and inquired if he was pleading guilty to three counts of negligent homicide, to which he simply stated, "Yes." Then the judge asked if he would like to say anything to the family of the deceased, to which he responded a shameless, "No." I saw no remorse whatsoever in his reaction. He simply appeared aggravated. I expect he realized he was finally going to serve time in prison. Whatever he felt, I had no sympathy for this cold-hearted man as I reflected back to the statement he had made when he saw my family in the wreckage.

The district attorney informed me that each year before the defendant would come up for parole, the prison would notify me of the hearing. He suggested each year I write a letter to the parole board telling them why I felt the prisoner should remain in prison, considering the severity of his crime and the minimal penalty he had received. I assured him I would write the letters; I definitely wanted to make certain he served at least the entire three-year term.

Approximately one year later, I received the first notice of his parole hearing, and I promptly wrote my letter. I was advised a few weeks later that his parole had been denied—he would serve another year. I felt a sense of relief and satisfaction. However, at the end of the second year, I did not receive a notice, so I called the prison office to find out why. The representative informed me the prisoner had been released several months before for good behavior. It was over. There was nothing else I could do. He was free!

The local television stations began calling me for an interview. At first, I refused saying it was over, and I didn't feel the need to discuss it any longer. They insisted the public deserved to know what had happened and how I felt about the events. A voice from within told me to do the interview, so I hesitantly agreed. The next morning, television vans pulled up in front of my home. I immediately began to feel nervous, almost nauseous.

In Ephesians 6:18, Paul tells us to "pray at all times, say quick brief prayers making this our habitual response to every situation we meet throughout the day." I didn't know what to say to the reporters. I knew I didn't want a judgmental attitude that would only serve to build myself up. I quickly prayed, and my response to the media's questions was within me. I knew what I had to do. I had to give resolution to the negative results I had received from the entire trial experience. I had to prove humans could not destroy my faith in God.

As I walked outside for the interview on my front lawn under an oak tree, the reporters instantly fired questions at me. When they asked how I felt about the injustice dealt to my family and me, I spoke with confidence.

My response was simple. I told the reporters, "There could never be enough prison time served to satisfy what I thought this man deserved. The system had indeed failed me; however, God would be the final, supreme judge. One day, this man will stand before my Father and be accountable for his crimes, and this was my only satisfaction here on earth. It had been two years since my loss, and I was placing all this behind me. I was moving on with my life. I refused to look back at what should have been accomplished here on earth to produce the justice my family deserved."

When I completed the interview, the reporters thanked me, and I felt tears rolling down my cheeks as I walked back inside my home. Just as Isaiah asked Jacob, "How he could say the Lord does not see his troubles, God gives power to the weak and strength to the powerless." (Isaiah 40:27) I knew at that moment by trusting in my Lord I would find a new strength, and I would soar with wings like eagles. I would run and not grow weary, and I would walk and not grow faint. I would trust the Lord to take over this situation and the remaining chapters in my life. I turned it over to Him so I would feel closure in the result of a trial here on earth. I prayed God would show me the way to forgive this man. Again, I would have to trust God to take care of my future.

In Hebrews, Paul details how many of the Old Testament prophecies had already been fulfilled. In his concluding words in his book, he taught what God had said, "I will never fail you, and I will never abandon you. So we can say with confidence, 'The Lord is my helper, so I will have no fear. What can mere people do to me?'" (Hebrews 13:5-6)

To this day, I occasionally have people ask if I know whatever happened to the man who caused the wreck. I can look them in the eye and honestly say I have never given him another thought since that day. God released me from my torment and taught me how to forgive, a priceless gift. With the Lord's help, I will never allow people to control my life with anger or bitterness.

Larry Hill & Janice (Clifton) Anderson, 1972
Valley View High School
"Most Likely to Succeed"

Texas State Track & Field Champion
After qualifying to compete in the State Meet,
Larry won First Place in the Shot Put & the Discus,
becoming the second boy from our high school to
ever win a state championship. The only other state
champions from our high school were my brothers,
who had placed 1st and 2nd in previous years.

Larry Hill, #36, 1972
Valley View High School Football Team
Larry was a star Full Back throughout our
high school years

Larry & me on our wedding day, January 12, 1974
Valley View United Methodist Church
My mother made my wedding dress, copying a
design I chose from a bridal magazine.

Mr. & Mrs. Larry Hill
Our wedding, with our parents, Sherman & Wanda
Clifton and Frances & Vernon Hill, 1974

Larry's first high school coaching position after
college graduation, 1977

Clifton Marlon Hill was on born October 24, 1976.
He was my blonde haired, blue eyed lovable little
boy. He loved sports and was destined to be an
athlete coming from such an athletic family.

Adrianne Marie Hill was born to us on May 19, 1978. She was our dark haired, brown eyed precious daughter who was the "apple of her daddy's eye".

Cliff & Adrianne, circa 1979, Celina, Texas
This has always been one of my favorite photos of my children.

Larry played "by ear" and was an excellent musician and singer. He always loved serenading his little girl as she danced to the rhythm of his music.

Adrianne & Cliff at one of their birthday parties, circa 1981, in Sanger, Texas where Larry coached at the time.

Cliff & Adrianne, Easter, 1982, Sanger, Texas

Cliff after one of his first fishing trips with his dad. He was a typical boy, always playing hard, getting dirty, and having fun.

Larry and his brother, Ron, after one of many all night
fishing trips.

Adrianne & Cliff with their first dog, Shelly.
Cliff wanted to take pictures that night even though
he had been crying. Larry & I had just explained to
the children that Shelly was very sick and would not
be at the house when they came home from school
the next day.

Adrianne's first dance recital in Red Oak, Texas.

Cliff & Adrianne at my office in downtown Dallas.

The kids with their new puppies, Bonnie & Clyde at
our house in Petrolia, Texas.

Adrianne at her 8th birthday party, the last one
we celebrated.

Adrianne & Cliff while visiting Austin, Texas, only two months before the accident.

Mother & Daddy at my brother's home in Michigan, 1987

Mr. & Mrs. Robert Anderson
The intimate ceremony in our home on January 24,
1988 was the beginning of a new life for me and Bob.

Grandma Clifton celebrating her 100th birthday with her children, my Aunt Juanita Fern, Daddy and Aunt Margaret, 2001

Bob & me at our Pagosa Springs,
Colorado summer home, 2006

My oldest brother, David, and his family at Thanksgiving, 2011

My sister, Lisa, and her family, Christmas, 2010

My brother, Danny and his family in their home at
Christmas, 2010

CHAPTER 11

My Blessings Overflow

If we trust in God,
He will give us the power to be successful.
—Deuteronomy 8:18

In the days following the trial, my life gradually became more bearable. I had lived in apprehension of the trial for so long I did not realize I was becoming obsessed with its outcome. Satan attempted to initiate a war within me, but he had not won. I prayed to God before I spoke to the media, and He demonstrated that it was time to demand Satan get behind me. God knew how to win battles, and He proved it to me by teaching me the benefits of forgiveness. I demonstrated to God through prayer that my trust is in Him in every aspect of my lives, and I was reminded again how prayer must become the way I approach every situation in the future.

It did not take long for the next hurdle in my life to surface. I found myself facing the structure of my financial situation, something many of us seem to worry about simply because we fail to follow God's instructions. He will provide for our every need. Medical expenses mounted during the first two years, as I required multiple surgeries to repair damage in my abdomen. I was blessed my company's medical insurance provided very good coverage. My employer's life insurance paid me an accidental death benefit for my loss of Larry, I received a benefit from his teaching position, and my in-laws had taken out a small life insurance policy on each of our children at birth as a savings plan for their future college education. By no means had I imagined I would use my children's life insurance policies for death benefits instead of their college expenses. The man who caused the wreck had no insurance, so I received nothing outside of my own coverage.

Together, I received enough to help pay the remainder of my medical bills, enough to buy a reliable car, and place a little in savings, but I knew I would certainly have to work the rest of my life. I was only thirty-two; therefore, if I began putting money aside now, maybe I could retire someday. I was attentive and concerned about my financial situation, but it never proved a major concern to me. I remembered the scripture in Matthew 6:33, "Seek the Kingdom of God above all else, and live righteously, and he will give you everything you need." God would provide for all my needs. I would trust in Him for my financial well-being.

In Ecclesiastes 4:5, Solomon explains, "Fools fold their idle hands, leading them to ruin." I knew I had to remain busy as my life continued to move forward, for if I didn't, it would open the door for depression and loneliness. Though my body had not completely mended, I joined a health club and began exercising some evenings after work. I never before had the opportunity to work out in a gym. I was limited in the activities due to all my recent surgeries; however, I discovered water aerobics to be of great physical benefit. I loved the fluidity of the water and the gentle resistance it offered my recovering body. The water became a meditation time for me, and I found myself spending more and more time in the pool.

I also began to read books, a relaxation I had long forgotten. I could have counted on one hand the number of books I had read in the past twenty years; I just did not have or take the time to read. Daddy was an avid reader, and during this leisure pastime, we discovered a new interest between us. We shared books and spent endless hours discussing what we had read. We also found an interest in discussing the scripture and our varying generational interpretations of the Bible.

There had always been an artistic ability waiting to emerge within me, but I had never allowed it the time to develop. I became interested in painting and enjoyed taking classes to test my abilities. One day while visiting a friend's home, I asked her about a beautiful stained glass piece displayed in one of her windows. She told me she had made the piece in a class she had recently begun taking. It wasn't long until I joined her class, and I experienced another buried art form. I loved working with glass and found I could somewhat relate it to life. I would select a design I wanted to make and take my time going through each box of glass to find just the right shade, texture, and lines to complement the design. I learned to cut the pieces according to the pattern and carefully solder each one together to bring life to a beautiful work of art. There were times I would accidently break a piece of glass and have to find another, and there were times I would bleed when I did not properly handle the glass, but more important, I completed a project I created and of which I could be proud. I wondered if I had experienced a diminutive fraction of the satisfaction God enjoyed as He created the things here on earth; smiling with pleasure as He carefully placed each creation in its place. The magnitude of His joy would certainly have been unimaginable in our small minds.

Another interest of mine emerged. David and Marcia had given me a camera for my high school graduation. Remember the box-type cameras with the square flashcube on top that rotated after each flash picture? That simple camera influenced the rest of my life. I pray David and Marcia know what an inspiration that gift was to me.

Beginning with Larry and my high school graduation, our senior trip to Galveston, and continuing through our young married life together, I enjoyed taking pictures with that little camera. As our family grew, I was faithful in taking all the traditional photos at Easter, during birthdays, Thanksgiving, and especially at Christmastime. I treasure the twenty years of photos I had stored in boxes; they gave me a gift of memories that would last a lifetime.

My interest in photography was quickly renewed, and I began researching new camera technology and purchased my first advanced multi-lens camera. I found comfort in taking photographs of my new world, things I had never seen before. I began taking close-ups of flowers, old abandoned houses and barns, landscapes, and anything and everything that caught my attention. I was delighted to be seeing this world "through a new lens," so to speak. I began filling albums with photos, which seemed to provide a sort of comfort to me as my life continued.

I recall showing Mother and Daddy my latest developed photographs one weekend. Daddy laughed and with a little grin he said, "Let me get this right. You stopped on the side of a highway, climbed over a fence, and walked through a pasture to take a picture of that old, run-down barn and a fence post?" Knowing he might have believed I was losing my mind, I simply answered, "Yeah! But look how cool that old barn is!" He just shook his head, looked at Mother, and then smiled at me. I could always make my daddy smile! I think through my new hobby I may have brought a fresh visualization into his and Mother's life, as they seemed to enjoy looking at my photos, or maybe it was just that they could see the enjoyment photography was bringing into my life.

One weekend, I gathered and carried boxes of photographs to my parents' house; photos I had collected from the past twenty years. Some of them were arranged haphazardly in albums, but most were stuffed into various envelopes and boxes, and no dates, names, or places on a single one. Mother and I sat at her dining room table for several weekends going through every photograph and making little stacks that represented times and places. But more importantly, we looked at each picture—remembering, crying, and talking about our memories. It was a healing time for us both. Eventually, we managed to organize each photograph in an album, preserving each visual memory deep within our hearts.

My photo albums began filling shelves throughout the next few years. I came to recognize photography had become a valuable escape for me; it had also become a way to preserve memories, a precious commodity during that time in my life. Memories are the one thing in life no one can take from me. Once we have them, they are ours to keep. What a treasured gift!

Today, I continue to enjoy photography and all the new technologies. I store every photo, not in hardback photo albums, but electronically, and I categorize them by year, occasion, location, and people, so that when I want to reminisce visually, I can immediately go to that file. Invariably, a photo will bring back a special memory and a smile mixed with an occasional tear.

Photography also gave me a new respect for the beauty of this earth, something too many of us take for granted. If we allow God into our lives, the amazing splendor that surrounds us will carry a brand new appreciation, and we will realize we must praise God every single day for our environment. I now know the true meaning of the term, "Take time to smell the roses." We should all take, or should I say, make time to smell the roses!

I remember on Sunday mornings when I was a young girl, Daddy would put on his suit and go out to Mother's rosebushes in the flowerbeds surrounding our house. Many times, I would help him look over each bush to find the perfectly opened bud. Once found, he would use his ever-present pocketknife to cut the stem against his calloused thumb, smell the bud, and then pin it on the lapel of his suit jacket. He would then pick up his tattered, well-used Bible and begin the block-long walk down the street to our church. He never asked anyone to walk with him, for this was his time to meditate and prepare his mind for the class he was about to teach. My daddy's favorite flower was obviously the rose, and after years of study, I now understand a possible reason why he favored them so much.

Throughout the Bible, there are many references to the rose, which I believe represent Jesus. In the Song of Solomon, Solomon has dialogue between himself and a simple Jewish maiden, wherein the young woman describes herself, "I am the rose of Sharon, and the lily of the valley." (Song of Solomon 2:1) She explained she was not special at all, but was as common as the flowers in Israel.

The charming, witty, petite author of *All Cracked Up*, Patsy Clairmont tells of her love for the rose and its fruitful existence in the book, *Patchwork Devotional*. I love her keen description of a rose.

> It begins as a bud, which has beauty all its own; gracefully unfolds into velvet overlays; and then, with its last breath, when crushed, it leaves a heady fragrance and drips precious oil. Okay, there is the thorn issue, but in the overall scope of flower life, the rose is the reigning queen.

> As we consider the beauty and grace of the rose, we're not surprised to discover that Jesus is called the Rose of Sharon. He was born a bud of a babe in a manger; his beauty unfolded before others with each humble step he took; and in his last breaths on earth, with thorns pressed into his head, after being crushed by our sins, he shed precious drops of his blood and released a forever fragrance of love. In the overall scope of our life, Christ is our coming King.

> That sacrifice, Christ's broken body, now calls us to receive the crushing blows of life as a way for his fragrance to be released through us. Our crushed and drooping lives become a holy potpourri. Take a shattered heart, mix with a crushed spirit,

intermingle with Christ's oil of mercy, stir with his healing touch, and season with divine love. What a magnificent fragrance.

Think of Patsy's description the next time you see a beautiful rose created by the hands of God. Oh, and by the way, don't forget to smell it as well. Smell the sweet scent of His work.

CHAPTER 12

Love is the Greatest

Three things will last forever—
faith, hope, and love—
and the greatest of these is love.
—1 Corinthians 13:13

Weekends were definitely family time among my friends. My friends were very considerate and often insisted I join them, but I never really felt comfortable. In fact, I actually found groups or families would sometimes intensify my loneliness. So for several months, I continued traveling to my parents' house on weekends to keep from feeling so alone, and I think it actually seemed to bring them joy as well.

As the end of 1986 approached, I began to feel anxious about the impending holidays and how strange I would feel during this time without my husband and children. But God made His presence known once again. Some very dear friends invited me to accompany them on a ski trip during the holidays. We would fly to Colorado the day after Christmas and stay in a condominium for several days. We would ski, enjoy the beautiful snowy mountain scenery, cook, share our meals, and play games, laugh, and fellowship together in front of a warm fireplace. What an answer to my prayers!

However, to quote a good friend, I can officially say I have been skiing twice in my life, "the first and last time." I enrolled in a beginner's lesson, and after the class, made my first trip to the top of the mountain. I remember praying, "God, if you get me off this mountain, I promise I will never try this again!" He did, I didn't, and that's that, my first and last time! It's funny how we tend to make deals with God when we need His help. I was definitely willing to negotiate anything as I began my first trip down what I considered a treacherous mountainside. I quickly learned that skiing requires abdominal muscle strength, something I had never really developed in the first place, and what little I did have was lost when my seat belt crushed my abdomen in the wreck. The six months prior to our ski trip, I had not only endured the intense emotional stress of the accident, but I had also undergone two major and two minor surgeries. I quickly learned snow skiing was not my forte, and I was definitely not physically prepared for the sport.

Despite my poor skiing skills, I had a most enjoyable but bittersweet time during the week. I will never forget the kindness my friends shared and the diversion it provided me during the holidays. It was my first Christmas without my husband and children, but with my friends' help in keeping my body busy with the challenging aches and pains of skiing, I discovered it was the best thing I could have possibly done during that time. I will never forget their kindness and unselfish love they shared with me during that holiday season.

Present within me was a new courage to experience things I would have never tried in my previous life. I made the choice to become a better person, instead of turning into a bitter old woman, which would have been easy. A new world opened for me the year following the wreck. There is the life you learn from and the life you live, and I wanted to gain something from the tragic life I had already experienced and become the new person God had placed within me.

I gradually became more socially active. I did many things because I felt brave, and I knew was an answer to my prayers. God met me with strength in my weaknesses. I learned to take pleasure in the various cultural and social events throughout the city. I enjoyed the company of a few male friends on occasion, but found no one with whom I could seriously connect. I wasn't even certain I wanted to connect with anyone. I was still mourning the loss of my husband, and as many people feel who have lost a spouse, I felt uncomfortable, as if I was cheating on Larry. I knew in my heart Larry would want me to go on with my life, but he was the only man I had truly ever loved or been with, and it just didn't seem right. I trusted God would show me when the time was right, so I never worried about what my future held, and I remembered what my boss said, "Take it one day at a time."

My coworkers were very good listeners and most showed genuine concern in how my life was progressing. I quickly developed an attribute that I now know is one of precious value; I learned to listen. I realized the greatest necessity in a friendship or a relationship is the priceless skill of listening. Listen with your heart, listen to others, and listen to what life is telling us. Listening makes our hearts grow bigger, which enables us to be of help to others and their needs. I heard in a sermon that many of us suffer from "love blindness." The pastor explained that love blindness is when we are deficient in love and ignore others because of whom or what we perceive them to be. He said by choosing to love all people, regardless of who they are, we could cure the symptoms of loneliness, lack of drive, and discontentment. I wanted that cure!

In my office, I listened to one coworker speak of the latest dilemmas she was encountering with her young teens. I couldn't help her or give her advice, but I could listen, which seemed to be all she wanted. A younger male coworker joked of his dating dilemmas, actually, more of his "lack of" dating dilemmas. Another man spoke of issues developing with his wife's aging parents. I listened to it all and embraced the interaction with each of them. I welcomed the steady stream of coworkers as they gathered almost daily in my office to talk, visit, and laugh. It was a much-needed distraction during that phase in my life.

Another person began talking to me privately about problems he was encountering in his marriage—my boss, Bob. I had worked with Bob's wife before I had accepted the position I presently held, so I knew her almost as well as I knew him. I felt somewhat uncomfortable talking to him about his relationship because after all, he was my boss. There were times when I would end up discussing things with him and his wife over dinner at their home. I sympathetically listened to both, wishing I could help resolve their differences, but it was obvious there were some deep-rooted issues between them.

I was raised in a home where we were taught marriage was meant for life and with the proper help and a desire to resolve issues every couple could work out their differences. Bob and his wife did not resolve their differences, and it wasn't long until he moved out of his home and into an apartment. It all seemed to happen quickly. She filed for an amicable divorce, moved out of town, and Bob moved back into his home.

Anyone around our office could tell Bob had not been happy for some time. A year or so before, when the entire office helped him celebrate his fortieth birthday, I remember a comment he made to several of us during the party. He asked if any of us had ever wondered if this was all there was to life; was this as happy as we would ever be? He didn't say it in a joking manner, even though most of us responded that way. He was seriously asking us if we believed this was it. I remember thinking at the time what a very sad and depressing thing to say. However, I gradually began to understand he was indeed very unhappy in his present life, and he wanted something more out of it. I certainly didn't know why he felt so unhappy, and I'm not sure he even knew; he simply believed there was something missing in his life. All these feelings may have been the male, mid-life crisis syndrome we hear about, but whatever it was, it was obvious to all of us he was not happy.

Bob had been a good friend and a compassionate listener for me during my struggles. I felt obligated to return the favor by listening to him; I felt sorry for him. He had been there for me as far back as when he would come to my parents' house and take me for rides, and patiently listen to me while I tried to make decisions in my life. Now he was obviously distraught and needed a friend.

Bob and I began spending more and more time together, and we became really good friends. There had never been anything romantic about our relationship from the very beginning. I considered him my boss and my friend and that was all. As far as I knew, he felt the same way. As the months went by, Bob and I continued having long conversations and found we enjoyed each other's company. Then one day as we were returning from lunch and talking as usual, he suddenly pulled the car over and stopped. He reached over and kissed me. I was stunned, embarrassed, and a little perturbed he had made such an advance.

It had been a very long time since I had been kissed the way he kissed me. We didn't really discuss what had happened during that time, but it was just a matter of days until he confessed his love for me and admitted he had known he loved me for some time. I couldn't believe what I was hearing! Had I been oblivious to what was happening? Was I so self-absorbed in my own life that I hadn't recognized his feelings for me? I knew things were unsettled in his life, and he probably needed time to work out some issues with his recent divorce.

I wasn't even sure I was ready for a relationship. I certainly didn't know if I loved him. We were good friends, and maybe that was all I really needed right now. I was concerned he could be on the rebound from his marriage, or maybe he was the kind of man who just didn't ever want to be alone. There were many uncertainties about him. He had confided in me about his personal life, things of which I did not necessarily approve. But there was this strange, uncomfortable feeling within me. I never had anyone tell me how much he loved me and me not being able to respond in the same way. I was flattered, and yes, I did love him, but not in the manner in which he implied. I was very confused with all these new developments in my life.

Shortly after this happened, I visited with the pastor at my parents' church and spoke to him about Bob, my concerns, and the advances he had made toward me. The pastor pointed out that it had been more than a year since my loss, and it was natural for me to move on with my life. He cautioned me to make sure Bob had determined he made the right decision in his life by divorcing his wife before we allowed any further relationship to develop. He also expressed concern about my emotional state. Was I ready for a relationship? I knew God and I, together, were the only ones who could truly answer that question.

Pastor even asked me if I felt threatened in my job by Bob's advances. It was at this point in our conversation that I realized I had not felt threatened at all. In fact, I suddenly began defending Bob. Maybe I really did like him more than I thought I did. Pastor helped me understand I was presently at the point in my life where, if I wanted to, was acceptable for me to fall in love again, if not with Bob, with someone else. He gave me much to think and pray about. I did not take his suggestions lightly, and I remembered Matthew 6:24, "God must be our first love." I knew I had received the blessing of God's love, and I had placed Him at the forefront of my life. Now I felt there was someone who could become my second love.

Our new developing relationship weighed heavily on my mind for some time. I let Bob know about my pastor's advice, and we decided to allow our relationship to develop gradually, and one day at a time. I spoke to my parents about Bob, and they did not seem surprised about our affections toward each other. They told me they had gained great respect for

Bob throughout my recovery. They recognized he obviously cared about me and were not surprised to learn the extent of his caring. If Bob made me happy then it would make them happy; that was how they left it with me.

As my relationship with Bob continued to develop, I remember telling my two brothers about him. David, my oldest brother's first response was to express his concerns about Bob being more than forty years old, several years older than I was, and that he was divorced. Jokingly, yet seriously, I told him I'd rather have a forty-year-old man who had been married and divorced, than one who had never been married. At least Bob knew what he was getting into.

However, when I told Danny, his response totally shocked me. He said he knew Bob had loved me for a long time. What? How did he know? He really didn't even know Bob! He asked me if I could remember the day after the wreck when Bob visited me in the hospital. Danny said he had spoken to Bob for some time that day, and he recognized Bob had feelings for me, he just didn't know to what extent. I told him I remembered when Bob came to the hospital, and how odd I thought it was he had driven that far just to stand by my bedside for a few minutes.

My sister's reaction was one of absolute surprise, and she made me sit down and tell her all about my new relationship. It was as if we were back in high school talking about boyfriends, first dates, and kisses. She was extremely happy for me as well.

Some time later, I too was curious and asked Bob why he had driven two hours to come to the hospital the day after the wreck. He explained that all the office coworkers were sitting around mournfully talking about the results of the accident, and he said he couldn't handle the intense emotion of sorrow he was feeling. He got in his car and began driving with no destination in mind. The next thing he knew, he was pulling into the hospital parking lot. He said he felt sorry for me, and he wanted to see me and express his sympathy.

Other than those things, he said he couldn't explain why he had come or what he was feeling. I believe his steps were unknowingly guided from above that day.

I have to admit, I continued to have some reservations about our budding relationship. For the first time in my life I was on my own and becoming familiarized with my lifestyle. But I began to wonder. Did I want to be alone, possibly for the rest of my life? How many eligible men my age were out there with whom I would be interested, or even worse, would be interested in me?

Larry had been a big, rough, tough athletic type, who enjoyed hunting, fishing, and contact sports. Bob, on the other hand, was of a much smaller stature, indeed the exact physical opposite of Larry. He liked sports, but mostly on television, and he preferred golf to any other outdoor activity. Raised in seaport cities, he spent his youth involved in water sports. What a contrast! The differences in their physical statures didn't matter to me, but one thing I easily recognized as similar characteristic qualities in the two men I loved in my life, they both possessed integrity, a trait I very much admired. They deeply loved, accepted, and encouraged me to be my own person.

Larry and I led a humble life with teacher and secretarial salaries and two small children. We never seemed to have much money, but still we were extremely happy together. From the start, we had always wanted children, and as most young college students, we couldn't afford to have them, but did anyway, trusting in our faithfulness of God. A chance we took and never regretted.

My social life with Larry and our children consisted of every athletic event offered at the school, as well as our own children's activities. We didn't have time for a social life outside of this realm. We had many friends, but they were all associated with the school system and parents of our children's friends. As I look back, I wonder how I had time for everything, as I'm sure many young mothers feel even more so today. But I accomplished it, as so many others do. I drove a long distance and worked an eight-hour day at the office, came home, prepared dinner, rushed through a load or two of laundry, bathed and put the kids to bed, and collapsed until the next morning when it all began again.

I had questions and many concerns about being involved with Bob, as we were very different. He chose divorce; I did not choose to lose Larry or my kids. I had been very happy in my marriage, and all I had left were memories. I could not stop reminiscing about things that had happened, but I was somewhat concerned if it would trouble Bob if I continued to talk about my memories as I had in the past. There were so many questions, and then Bob asked the big question. He asked me to marry him! Our relationship had slowly progressed, and we both knew we wanted to spend the rest of our lives together. I said yes, and the next level of questions began popping into my mind.

Bob was mid-level management in a very large company and made a very nice salary. If we married, I would not be able to keep my job since I was a direct report of his, and our company's policy did not allow for such a working arrangement. Bob wanted to retire when he was fifty-five. What would that be like? I even had some concern about him being divorced. If we ever experienced problems, would he consider divorce as his first course of action? Bob and his wife never had children, and he had already told me he didn't want to start a family at his age. I didn't know if I would be physically capable of having more children since I had endured so many internal injuries in the wreck, but I would want to explore my options before making such an important decision.

Neither of the men in my life had been extremely religious, but then I had not been either. We had all grown up in the church, but as unfortunate as it is, like many young married couples, we had let our active church life wane. I had always known God, but never fully understood what having Him in my life as a friend would mean to me. I felt I had become somewhat emotionally stable for more than a year now. I encountered a few minor breakdowns, but I felt I was well on my way to recovery. I realized later I had already started to let my dependency on Christ diminish somewhat as life became easier for me. I had not needed God as desperately as I had before. However, as I began to pray for guidance in my decisions, there He was again! He was waiting for me to come back to Him. This time I was not begging for His help, I simply needed His direction. Were all these things happening in my life His plans for me, or was I trying to make my own plans and decisions by myself?

God again answered my prayers and showed me that Bob and I were meant for each other. Bob and I were married in a small, intimate ceremony in our home on the day of my thirty-fourth birthday, almost a year and a half after I lost my family. My daddy once again gave me away as we walked down a center aisle between white wooden chairs arranged in our small living room. My sister was matron of honor, and Bob's best man was a friend from work. The best man played the guitar, and with his wife, harmoniously sang the beautiful songs we had chosen. There were only a few close friends and family invited to the private wedding, but more than a hundred friends and family attended the reception to help us celebrate the beginning of our new lives together. We felt everyone's joy and happiness, and we knew God had truly given us His blessings that day.

The pastor whom we asked to marry us, had just months before performed the funeral for my family and had later counseled me on my developing relationship with Bob. During our ceremony, the pastor spoke about the experiences Bob and I had been through prior to our relationship and how blessed we were to have become such good friends before we married. As he spoke, I heard my mother and daddy crying softly as they sat behind me. Tears welled up in all our eyes as we repeated our vows to love, honor and obey, until death do us part.

I better than anyone in the room knew about death and parting. I had loved and lost, and my childhood dreams were over. I was much more mature than I had been at nineteen when I married Larry, but still, there was something familiar. I had now married two men in my life, and I respected and deeply loved both of them. Bob and I did not know what our future held just as Larry and I did not know either. But what Bob and I knew at that moment was God had placed us together at a time in our lives when we desperately needed each other. We were extremely happy and ready to start our lives in the presence of our Lord, Jesus Christ.

CHAPTER 13

Hold My Hand, Dear Friend

The Lord directs the steps of the godly.
He delights in every detail of their lives.
Though they stumble,
they will never fall,
for the Lord holds them by the hand.
—Psalm 37:23-24

Bob and I began our life together as would any newlyweds. We were both joyful and did not want to spend a minute apart. I resigned my position and became a self-employed secretary. My first position was a temporary, part-time job with a privately owned oil company in the same building where Bob continued to work. My job lasted two years, so much for temporary!

When Bob and I first began dating, one evening as we were sitting in a beautiful restaurant in downtown Ft. Worth, he asked me if I thought I could get used to this kind of lifestyle. I laughed at such a ridiculous question, of course, I could! Before I could answer him aloud, he continued to tell me he hoped I would, because he had many more adventures planned for us. Our adventures began with a honeymoon cruise and several subsequent cruises within the next few years. He told me we were just beginning, and he has never disappointed me on the promise he made to me that evening.

We soon purchased a small motor home and on weekends began traveling to nearby places. We loved the entire camping experience, except I hadn't known this kind of camping. I had only camped in tents with my family's last trip in a tent camper, which at that time we believed was the ultimate in pure luxury. Bob joked that his idea of roughing it was leaving the television remote control at home! We both took pleasure in the outdoors, and we found a common interest in traveling and exploring new places.

Every chance we had we spent time exploring new and unfamiliar places in the states around us, and it wasn't long until we wanted to travel more extensively. One of our first long road trips was to visit his parents' home near Tampa, Florida. We were grateful to be able to spend time there and for me to get to know his parents. I quickly discovered where Bob had gotten his wonderful sense of humor and fun loving mannerisms—his parents. I was nervous about them accepting me, but it wasn't long until I felt comfortable with them in their home.

Bob was offered a new position in Midland, Texas, shortly after we married. The company flew us to Midland, and we found a newly constructed home ready to purchase. Before we knew it, the movers had us packed and ready to leave the town that held a multitude of memories for both of us. During the excitement of the final moving day, Bob received a phone call informing us his father had passed away; succumbing to the throat cancer he had suffered from for some time. Of course, this news turned our excitement rather sorrowful as we mourned his father's death, but had to continue with the packing. Bob suffered from the overwhelming loss of his father. He had always been very close to his dad, and he took the loss very hard. He had lost his best friend.

Losing Bob's dad was a sad way for us to begin our life in a new city, and we discovered it was not going to be as blissful as newlyweds might expect. We dealt with the continuing problems relating to the divorce, something we prayed would end and eventually did. My body had healed from the surgeries, but now I began experiencing monthly pain in my abdomen, and a short time after our move to Midland, I was required to have a hysterectomy. We approached this surgery with trepidation. Even though Bob and I had already decided we were not going to have children together, I faced this finality apprehensively.

I cannot explain the emotion a mother feels when she loses a child. I had a strong, deep-seated fear of losing another child, and I could not face the possibility of suffering through another loss of that magnitude. I will always miss having children, my children, but I know in my heart that God directed Bob and me to make the right decision at this time in our lives. In my life now, many of my friends are enjoying their grandchildren, something I regretfully will never experience. I have never felt jealous of other families and the happiness they have, in fact, I feel the exact opposite. I am extremely joyful to see other's happiness. I guess the best way to explain my emotions is that I will always suffer from my loss. I don't know any other words to describe it. The loss of my own children created a new passion within me, one of a deep spiritual love for all children. My loss made me very much aware of the fragility of their lives. I know God intends for us to celebrate the joys of His people and the miracle of children. I am blessed to have many children in my life, and I treasure all of them as if they were my own.

~~~

Bob's new job in Midland changed our lives dramatically. The position involved a marketing aspect, requiring him to travel and become more socially involved entertaining company clients. The oil industry was at an elevated peak in the oil-rich, Midland-Odessa area. The company paid for us to join a very nice country club in which to entertain clients. Bob played golf since high school, so many of our activities revolved around the golf club. Bob encouraged me to take golf lessons from the club professional. He said his dad taught him never to try to teach your wife to drive a car or to play golf, so he happily paid a professional to take on the challenge. This strategy proved beneficial in more ways than we could ever know. I enjoyed the game of golf and began playing three to four times a week, walking the golf course with girlfriends during the week, and playing as couples on the weekend.

The company provided us with season tickets to the Midland Theatre and box seats at the Midland minor league baseball team games. The company requested Bob and I plan a trip for a customer, which resulted in us flying to Cabo San Lucas to make the preparations. We arranged for a private jet and a charter fishing boat to take the executives of both companies deep-sea fishing. Twice a year, we wined and dined in Santa Fe, New Mexico, at an oil and gas conference, played in corporate golf tournaments, and dined at very expensive, fashionable restaurants. Bob's position required him to attend business conferences at the company's headquarters in Long Beach, California, and often meetings and boondoggles all over the country. Many times, it would be possible for me to travel with him allowing us both to enjoy the trips.

These were not the type of activities I was accustomed to in my prior life. For the first time in my life, my clothes closet literally had more formal wear than work clothes. Bob had certainly told me the truth when he said I should get used to the new life he had planned for us. I was living a life I had never dreamed possible; it was similar to a fairy tale.

Unfortunately, every so often a situation would shock me back into the reality of my past life. I remember one evening at a country club dinner party. I was visiting with several of the young wives we were entertaining, and they began complaining about their children. I tried taking part in the general conversation—you know, trying to fit in—when one of them asked me if Bob and I had children. When I simply told her no, they all began telling me how lucky we were that we did not have children. What a reality check for me! I sat there a moment not knowing what to say. Then I interrupted them and told them I had lost both my children in a car accident. One or two of them told me they were sorry, but then they immediately returned to their conversation oblivious to the hurt they had caused. They just didn't get it! I withdrew the rest of the evening and decided from that point on I would be more selective with whom I shared this information. For years, I never told anyone except my very closest friends. I didn't want people to feel sorry or awkward around me, and I certainly didn't want to feel what I had felt that night. My past life became my little secret.

~~~

By far the best thing that came out of Bob paying for me to take golf lessons was that I met one of the, no ... let me rephrase that, the best and most wonderful friend anyone could ever imagine. Her name was Kathy. She was a gracious, elegant, caring woman, and we quickly became dear friends. We walked and played golf, lunched and shopped together several times a week. She had lived an interesting life herself, and even though she was a few years older than I was, we became very close friends. Our husbands would join us on the weekends, and we would play golf, travel, and enjoy many social activities together, a pleasant experience outside the realm of work.

Kathy and I very much enjoyed each other's company, but we learned we had something else in common, something less fortunate. Kathy's father and mother were in poor health. In the book of James it is said, "Every good gift and every perfect gift is from above ...." (James 1:17) Kathy was my perfect gift at the perfect time. I needed God's help. I held His hand by way of my friend's hand, and through Kathy, I learned to deal with a situation that would soon develop with my own parents.

I missed being with my parents when we moved to Midland. Mother and I had always been very close, and we enjoyed doing things together. After the wreck, we would call each other daily. Mother and Daddy had never traveled much, but they soon learned they could hop on a flight from Dallas to Midland and be at our home in an hour. It was exciting times for me to have them stay overnight because I had always lived close enough where they could make day trips to visit. Until this point, they had never spent a night in my home.

On one of their visits to Midland, Daddy confided in me that Mother was beginning to forget things. I had noticed Mother repeating herself each time I spoke to her on the phone, but I had not thought much about it. After all, she had four children and she probably couldn't remember to whom she had told what. I feared the worse and selfishly could not fathom the thought of her not being there for me to talk to. My mother and I had become dear friends during the past few years, and I couldn't imagine life without her.

Kathy became my consultant on handling issues that unfortunately developed quickly with Mother. I would call Mother nearly every day and almost immediately, I realized how she was indeed confused on details. I was extremely disturbed once while visiting their home. Mother and I went to visit my cousin's new baby. My parents had lived within a few miles of Valley View their entire life, and when I asked her where to turn, I realized she was confused on which road to take to a town less than ten miles away from her home—a road she had traveled often for more than sixty years. I knew then this was not something Daddy or I were imagining. Mother did not severely worsen for a couple of years, but the condition was obvious to all the family that she was developing dementia, and we knew it would only get worse with time.

CHAPTER 14

His Tremendous Strength

*Listen carefully to the thunder of God's voice
as it rolls from His mouth.*
—Job 37:2

There was an old saying in the oil business that employees moved every three years. If not, their wives would have to clean house. I was to that point; I hated to vacuum! Bob was reaching the age he wanted to retire but was offered a position in Bakersfield, California. We discussed our options, and on the morning Bob left for the office to inform his boss he wanted to take the enhanced retirement package, he called me and said we needed to talk. Oh no! He told me his boss would not accept his retirement resignation until we flew to California to look around and consider the move.

We flew to California and immediately fell in love with the area where we would live. Bakersfield receives a bad rap for being located in the agricultural valley of southern California where it is extremely hot and dry in the summer and foggy and damp in the winter. But for some reason, to us the area seemed much like west Texas only surrounded by a beautiful mountain range and just a couple of hours from the wonderful

beaches of southern California. We immediately returned to
Midland, accepted the job, placed our house on the market on
a Monday, and sold it on Wednesday. I didn't have to vacuum
but once! I took this as a sign from God that we were making
the right move.

Bob and I built our first house together in Bakersfield. We
were in a new subdivision out in the country across from a
huge carrot field. It was a true California house: white stucco,
red tile roof, numerous massive windows, lush landscape, and
a beautiful glistening pool and waterfall in our backyard. We
moved into our house and the first weekend in it, Bob's company
required him to attend the Bakersfield Business Conference.
We had never heard of this conference, and honestly, he really
didn't want to go. But that afternoon he called me from the
convention; he was in complete awe of the event. More than
twelve thousand attendees had paid hundreds of dollars each
for a ticket. Bob went on to tell me the entire speaker lineup
was filled with major entertainers, past presidents, Apollo
astronauts, famous athletes, and world-renowned musicians.
He was so excited about the experience that he made sure I
attended the event in years to come.

Bob and I loved Bakersfield. We enjoyed the surrounding area
more than we even expected. Bob, born in Tampa, Florida, grew
up on the East Coast in Brunswick, Georgia, near St. Simons
Island, and attended the University of Georgia. He joined the
Navy that stationed him in San Diego, California, and Norfolk,
Virginia. He spent some time living in Galveston, Texas, with
his parents, and when his father retired, they moved to St.
Petersburg, Florida. He was very much a lover of the ocean. I
grew up in north Texas, not exactly coastline, and I had only seen
the ocean once in Galveston during my high school senior trip.
Bob and I took every opportunity to drive to the beaches along
the California coast, especially during the intense summer heat.
The beaches were definitely a favorite of ours, but we also loved
the mountains. We would take mini-vacations to a beautiful
mountain lake surrounded by towering pine trees.

We experienced all the California touristy things: Disneyland, Hollywood, Rodeo Drive, tours of movie stars' homes, Walk of Fame, and on and on. We attended the Pebble Beach Pro-Am Golf Tournament where we obtained autographs from famous people such as a new golfing sensation who had just appeared on the golf tour, Tiger Woods. We also saw world-renowned golfers such as Arnold Palmer and Jack Nicholas. Actor Kevin Costner had just completed the movie *Tin Cup*, and I behaved like a silly, giggly schoolgirl when he autographed my program and told me he liked my pen and asked if he could keep it. I think I said yes, but I really don't remember!

The first month we lived in our new home, I learned about a weather phenomenon that occurs in Bakersfield every fall. It's called Tule Fog. One morning I awoke and stepped outside the front door to pick up the paper only to realize I could not see across the street due to the dense fog. I had been exposed to this type of weather before, so I knew it would burn off later in the morning and might not occur again for several days. Well, it burned off all right, but it took three months, literally! There would be days we would go without seeing our neighbor's house. It was a tremendously thick and heavy fog, which made driving extremely dangerous. It was so frightening, I found myself afraid to go anywhere. Every night on the news, I watched stories of several major accidents caused by the foggy weather, and I became extremely depressed.

Since we had just moved into our new neighborhood, I did not know anyone around us, and during the day, I was literally home alone. Bob would go to work and be able to leave the valley. He would travel over the mountains and receive a sense of relief from the gloom that lay upon us for months. I was stuck at home, afraid to drive, and I did not know anyone. He thought it was extremely funny to call me from the mountaintop. He would rub it in how he could see the sun and the blanket of fog looming across the valley. I did not think it was nearly so hilarious.

One day, a Welcome Wagon woman knocked on my door. Oh, I was so happy to visit with someone whom I would normally not allow in the house. She told me about all the deals I would receive as a new resident, and she mentioned a Newcomer's Club in town. After several more weeks of the fog, I was desperate to visit with other women. I decided I had to do something, so I joined the club, which introduced me to other women who were also new to the area. This helped me become involved in social activities, and I developed many friendships within the club membership, many of whom I am still friends.

Bob and I settled into our new surroundings and enjoyed many activities with friends and neighbors. With so many new and exciting things to do in California, we never seemed to have the time to attend a church regularly. I understand now, that in some ways, the group of friends in the Newcomer's Club became like a church to us. The same theory on which this club was founded, is exactly the reason churches were developed back in the days of the Bible; it was designed for fellowship and learning. We were all new to the Bakersfield area, didn't know anyone, and needed friendship, so we were there for one another, not so unlike the original biblical concept of a church. We learned that many of our new friends were Christians, which enabled us to share a Christ-like relationship with them; I do believe God was there with us.

Shortly after I joined Newcomers, a woman whom I had recently met discovered her grandson was suffering from a rare medical illness. As a group, we prayed for healing, but the young boy passed away soon afterward. I felt such a loss for this dear, heartbroken woman, but I did not know what to do for her. Having been in her position of losing a small child, I wanted to reach out and console her, as my heart wept for her. I felt I didn't know her well enough to pick up the phone and call, so I did what I felt was the appropriate thing. I sent her a card that expressed my sorrow. As I sat one afternoon preparing the envelope to mail the card, I decided to write her

God, Help Me!

a note. I wanted to try to explain how I had experienced her pain and that it would eventually ease. I also wrote how she would have to rely on God to get her through her mourning.

My brief note turned into a several page letter, but I hesitantly folded the letter and placed it in the envelope. I feared she would think I was some kind of "Jesus freak" or something, but I knew in my heart she needed to hear the things I had written. So I sent it. It wasn't long before I received a phone call from the woman who, through her tears, thanked me for taking the time to share my life experience with her. She told me it had helped her tremendously in dealing with her loss, and she had even given it to her daughter, the young boy's mother, to read. Years later, while shopping in another state, I ran into this woman. We could not believe we were both at the same place at the same time, a thousand miles away from where we had lived, but more importantly, she again mentioned how much my letter had helped her family and her in dealing with their loss.

God had been with me in the fog in Bakersfield and made me open the door to the woman who told me about a club. Do I think He had that phase of my life scripted? Probably so! I know this was the first time I had ever really helped someone spiritually, and it all seemed precise as it fell into place. Sure, I had done things for others who had lost loved ones. I had taken food, sent cards and flowers, and told them to call me if I could help, but this was different. I helped someone by telling her about our amazing God and the miracles He could perform within our lives if we only allow Him to live within us.

In Matthew 10:42, it says, "And if you give even a cup of cold water to one of the least of my followers, you will surely be rewarded." God spoke to me that day, not just to write that letter, but also to reach out and share how He helped me, and yes, I was rewarded, even though that was not my reason for writing the letter. God blesses those who help others, and I was again blessed.

~~~

113

One of the negative things about having to move from town to town is leaving behind dear friends. Larry and I had moved several times in our thirteen years of marriage. It seems every year in the high school coaching business there is a prospective coaching position available somewhere. Larry was continually advancing his coaching career throughout our married life, which resulted in our moving at least four times after college. Similarly, it wasn't long after Bob and I left Midland that my dear friend Kathy and her husband moved to Houston with their company. We often spoke on the phone and sustained our long distance friendship very well. A few months after our California move, Kathy called and invited Bob and me to join them at a small campground in Pagosa Springs, Colorado. We were able to arrange for the visit, and for the next five years, we spent two weeks every summer there with them.

Our five years in California was brief, but we lived an exciting life there. Bob's company offered another enhanced retirement to their employees and this time Bob was fifty-three years old, and we leaped at the opportunity to retire. We felt we would be comfortable with what we had saved, and we were ready to make a significant change in our lives. However, as usual, what God had in store for us was not what we were planning. There is an old phrase that says if you want to make God laugh, tell Him your plans. He must have been laughing hysterically at this one!

We placed our house on the market, and it sold in just a few weeks. We sold much of our furniture, had a moving sale, and everything else we owned we packed away in a storage facility. The day arrived to leave our California home and the lyrics to "California Dreamin'" filled the air. We embraced each other as we began another of God's adventures He had planned for us. We vowed to each other to travel for at least a year before we decided where we wanted to settle down. We envisioned ourselves in a city with activities we had become so accustomed. For the next twelve months, we traveled across the country visiting quaint little towns and metropolitan areas, looking at homes, and trying to make our decision.

During a holiday visit to my parents in north Texas, Bob played golf with one of my uncles in a small community not far from where my parents lived. My aunt and uncle owned property there, which allowed them to play golf at the semi-private course. Bob returned that evening eager to tell me about the place, and long story short, we bought property in Nocona Hills, Texas, close to where I had grown up. At the end of our year of traveling, we began preparing to build our house. My first thought was, really? Out of all the places we could have lived, this was where we were going to end up? We traveled from coast to coast and explored some wonderful country, and we were going to move forty miles from my childhood home!

We would be thirty miles from the nearest big box store, not to mention fifty miles from anything else. This place was nothing like where we had expected to live out our lives. It was a rural area, way out in the country, and upon my sister's first visit, she asked if we had to grow our own food. It was not a country club; it was a club out in the country! The gated subdivision had a golf course, a nice lake, a clubhouse with a pool, and one little metal building near the gate that housed a church. The countryside was indeed beautiful nestled in a heavily wooded area covered with native oak trees on rolling hills surrounding the lake. All right, maybe this wasn't what we had in mind, but for some reason, we believed we were supposed to live there. I think this was the point where I could hear God giggling. God does giggle doesn't He? I suppose He does. Why wouldn't He take pleasure in a good giggle on occasion? I am certain we, as humans, continually do things to make Him laugh.

After our exciting year of traveling across the country, we parked our motor home in Mother and Daddy's extra lot next to their house. From there, we commuted daily to Nocona Hills working as we had never worked before. Our street,

Briarwood Trail, was named for a very good reason. There were briars covering every inch of our little acre. We began cutting the thorn-covered briars, trimming and cutting down several trees, and clearing the perfect area for our house. Many evenings we would build huge bonfires to get rid of all the brush. We sat around the fires in the evenings worn out from the physical labor of clearing brush and trees. Occasionally, we would even prepare dinner by the fire roasting hot dogs and marshmallows.

We would drive back to the motor home, shower, and collapse for the evening. I remember once when I was complaining to Bob about how tired I felt and he said to me, "Yeah, but isn't it a good tired?" I realized he was right. We were having fun doing entirely different things than we had ever done before. Where had all the fine restaurants gone that Bob promised me so long ago? But you know what? Before I realized it, I was perfectly content with our new life. We followed God's directions and knew we were where He had intended us to be.

Mother began to show signs of severe dementia and to add to her problems she developed Parkinson's disease. Daddy insisted on taking care of her at home by himself, but this was becoming an increasingly difficult burden on him at his age. With my siblings' constant insistence, he finally allowed me to help take care of Mother while we lived near their house in our motor home. When it came time for us to move into our home in Nocona Hills, Daddy was extremely tired, and the family finally convinced him to allow us to hire help for him. Mother passed away the next year, and Daddy became severely depressed. He remained so loving and caring for Mother during those last few months, but it had taken a toll on him.

Daddy, at the age of the age of eighty, was widowed, but the unusual thing about his life was he still had his own mother who was more than one hundred years old. Daddy and Grandma cared for each other emotionally, calling and talking at least twice a day. Grandma had never learned to drive, and probably would not have been driving at her age anyway. Daddy mourned the loss of his wife of more than sixty years, but his strong, petite Christian mother helped him recover as best she could. How amazing is that? For years, I told Daddy that Mother slipping away from us the way she did was God's way of preparing us for losing her. Nothing could ever completely prepare us for the loss, but we understood it was the right time for her to leave us.

Grandma lived another three years, and Daddy was struck with another devastating loss. I would go to Valley View to take him to lunch, doctor appointments, bookstores, and his favorite western wear store. We would generally spend the entire day together. At his request, we usually ended the day with a stop at a local ice cream shop for a hot fudge sundae or a banana split. At first, he would always suggest we share, but I don't ever remember eating quite as much as he did. He always did love his ice cream. I guess that's where I get my love for it as well!

One day while I was having lunch with Daddy, I noticed he didn't look well; he had a yellow tint to his completion. It was just a matter of weeks, after a routine doctor visit, that we were in absolute shock. We had known for years Daddy had prostate cancer, but the urologist felt that at Daddy's age it was under control, it was not spreading, and there was no need for further action. However, on this day the tests showed he had Stage 4 malignant cancer in his kidneys, liver, bladder, and part of his lungs. The doctor told us Daddy had approximately three months to live without treatments, and with extensive chemotherapy treatments, he could possibly extend his life a few additional months.

After fervent prayer, Daddy opted not to suffer through chemotherapy treatments and chose quality of life. He struggled with his choice, but our family agreed that whatever decision he made, we would support. After receiving such devastating news, Daddy bravely insisted we all continue to live our lives as normal as possible. Bob and I were in Pagosa Springs when I received a call informing me I needed to come home. I drove twelve hours straight and was there with Daddy the next day. Bob returned home the following day and came to be with my sister and me as we and hospice cared for Daddy. The doctors were correct; just three days after I returned to his side, Daddy passed away. As the doctor predicted, Daddy had lived almost exactly three months from when we learned about the cancer. He was now at peace with God and the people he loved most.

During the time of my mother and father's death, I received the news that my dear friend, Kathy, had developed a severe form of skin cancer. She was strong throughout her illness, never giving up hope for a cure, or ever showing defeat in her life. Bob and I were on our way to visit his mother in Florida when we received the call from Kathy's husband that she was gone. I will always consider Kathy my best friend in this world. We experienced many things together, and nothing will ever replace the friendship we shared. God had given me the gift of friendship, and I will always love her.

It seemed to me as if I was losing everyone. I had lost my husband and two children, Larry's father, then Bob's father, my mother, my best friend, my grandmother, and now my daddy. What was happening? Was this the way it was going to be the rest of my life, continue losing the ones I loved? How much more could I take?

CHAPTER 15

His First Commandment

You must not have any other god but me.
—Deuteronomy 5:7

R ecently, my sister, Lisa, pleaded with me to allow her to
read just the first chapter of this book. Despite my better
judgment, and against all teachings in regards to allowing
others to read unfinished work, I sent it to her with comments
that it was nowhere near completion. Even though I had the
confidence that God had given me the words to write, I still
worried others would not understand why I was writing this
book. This was Lisa's response after reading the first few
pages.

> Wow … I swallowed each word quickly like a
> starving man, and then I too soon came to the end
> and clamored to read more and more. Everyone who
> loves you has longed to hear the untold story of that
> fateful day, to share that which only you and God
> have shared for years now. Thank you for reaching
> deep within and pulling back memories that must
> still cut to your very soul. I believe the damage to
> your heart is done, it is finished, nothing can hurt

any more than that which you experienced, and the tragic wound has taken years to heal over enough for you to speak of it. Though forever scarred, God has patched you up as only He can and is now enabling you to tell your story.

I took the chapter out on my serene, secluded back porch to read, in private, where no one would see my reaction. I don't dare call you in person to tell you my thoughts; they are too tender. But I will say to you, "Get busy, and finish this book."

I could not call her either, for I sat crying at my computer reading the lovely comments and encouraging words she had written me. I did respond by e-mail and told her how grateful I was for her, her thoughts, and her encouragement. Lisa and I had always shared the special bond of sisterhood, but now I came to an understanding that she had been reluctant in speaking to me about the wreck. I then felt a renewed bond between us, not just our sisterhood in the flesh, but a more spiritual bonding.

I continued to explain to Lisa that I had always believed people, even family members, would rather not discuss the tragedy, and they probably felt uncomfortable bringing up the subject to me. I could not remember anyone really ever asking me anything about that day. I interpreted that as them not wanting to remember it. As I wrote in an earlier chapter, I felt they had continued with their own lives and remained somewhat unaffected by my situation. However, within a few months of my decision to write this book, I encountered several people who encouraged me to do so. My cousin's daughter, who was only nine years old when she spent the week at the lake with us before the wreck, told me last year, twenty-five years after the wreck, how that week changed her life forever. Yet, no one had ever asked me what I remembered or how I managed to live through it. God was showing me it was time to share my testimony with the world.

Lisa responded to my e-mail with the one below, which explains more to me than I could ever explain to anyone.

> You know it is odd, but I went years and years not even letting my mind go to a place that remembered that summer. And then one day a year ago, I was asked to lead a devotional at our church, and I felt led to use you as the focus. It was hard and I was trembling and I wasn't even sure that I could get through it, but an odd thing happened. It felt so good to say Larry, Cliff, and Adrianne's names again, aloud loud as if they were standing right next to me. I was comforted to hear their names spoken. I had missed saying them aloud, and I suddenly realized I was glad to be uttering their long lost names again. I wonder if you feel that when you are telling your story. It's good, isn't it, to feel their names roll off your lips?

> I will try to remember the devotional I gave that day or at least the gist of it. I began with the first commandment, "Thou shall have no other gods before me." I told the class how my interpretation of that verse had changed over the years. How once I viewed it as command from a jealous god who simply demanded to have top billing.

> So at that point in my devotional, I began to tell of your love story with Larry, your life, and the children you made together. There were several coaches in the audience and they could relate to the "Oh, so unique life of a Texas high school football coach and family." They were all smiling and really getting into the whole picture I painted for them. And then came the part of the story where they stopped smiling … the wreck. The bubble burst. In the blink of an eye!

> I told them that was when I saw clearly what God was doing when he gave us this commandment,

"Thou shall have no other gods before me." He wasn't being a jealous god at all, He was trying to protect us, guard our heart from devastation that would destroy us. He knew! He knows! He could see what mankind could not. Without placing Him above all else, we would be crushed by life, by the forces of life. Even our precious families, though precious even to God, could not protect us. After all, they could be gone in the blink of an eye. I saw Him then as a father trying to protect his foolish child from building his house on anything other than the rock that is God. God knew that He was all that we could depend on to be with us forever, to be there when life rolls over and crushes our very soul, and we *needed* to have no other gods or treasures before Him, for our own good, to survive in this world.

That is why you survived, Jan, because God was first and your family, though treasures, were second in your heart. YOU still had God! He cannot be, nor was He taken from you. God gave mankind a survival guide when He gave the world His first commandment. He didn't want to be king of the hill at all; He wanted to protect our souls from being crushed by the heel of life.

Once I gained my composure, I threw the empty box of tissues in the trash, and reread her message. My younger sister, Lisa, had seen something in my life that I had never recognized. It is a simple answer as to why I was able to survive my tremendous loss; why I was losing all the ones I loved.

Writers throughout the New Testament proclaim that even though God does not orchestrate our sufferings, He uses them to bring freedom at the deepest core of our being. I had walked with Him through all my suffering instead of blaming Him and pushing Him away, and He did amazing things in my life. I think that sometimes I was too close to my situation to understand things clearly. I knew I had suffered a tremendous loss, but I continued with my life without knowing how or why I was able to do what I had done. I knew God had helped me survive and thrive, but I didn't really know how. Lisa's e-mail describing her devotional to me explained how I had survived and thrived. I called out to God, asked for His help, and in return, He became the only god whom I worshiped. I certainly loved and missed my family for the rest of my life, but the moment God answered me as I laid there in the wreck, He became my rock, my redeemer, and the only constant in my life.

I came to recognize that it does not matter what we are going through in our life, if we obey that first commandment, God will be there for us at all times. No one on this earth, living in the flesh, will be able to say that to you. Human beings are going to make mistakes, bad mistakes, but our God never will. He wants us to worship and obey His commandments, and by doing so, He will never abandon us or give us any reason to doubt His love for us. He will always be our rock!

CHAPTER 16

Be Still and Listen

Jesus answered, "The wind blows wherever it pleases.
You hear its sound, but you cannot tell
where it comes from or where it is going.
So it is with everyone born of the Spirit."
—John 3:8

Bob and I had finally begun to understand how God completely controlled our lives. We did not know the purpose for which He had placed us in our new surroundings. However, it wasn't long until we came to realize that God intended us to be near my parents during their final years. They had been instrumental throughout my healing process, and now it was time for me to reverse the roles. God had given me another gift, the gift of sharing their last days, a gift that became ever so precious to me. Another void soon appeared in my life upon their passing.

Once again, my life began to change after I lost my parents. Bob and I continued living in Nocona Hills, playing golf and enjoying our new friends. We started attending the church in the little yellow metal building at the entrance of our community. Throughout our marriage, we had only been accepting God's blessings; we had never stopped to consider He might actually expect us to serve Him in some capacity. We became more and more involved in the church instead of the country club activities. It wasn't long until we recognized for the first time in our lives that we were doing something with real purpose for someone other than ourselves. Through our new church membership and fellowship with others, we began giving glory to God our Father.

Bob and I had each grown up in the Methodist Church, both joining our respective churches and accepting Christ during our teen years. We both knew God, but I don't think either of us knew what to expect when we began serving Him. We had not deserved the blessings God had given us throughout our lives, although we readily accepted and enjoyed each one. God could have said to us, "You have abandoned me and served other gods. So I will not rescue you anymore" (Judges 10:13), but through His mercy we came to recognize "that our Lord is greater than any other god" (Psalm 135:5).

Only about thirty members regularly attended our new church. We had come to know each one personally through golf and other social activities in the community. In a small way, we felt the church was still somewhat a social club, as the Newcomer's Club had been for me in Bakersfield. Church was a splendid way to meet new people and socialize. We soon developed strong Christian family relationships with many. But it didn't take long for us to see that church was more than a social activity.

The same pastor had been in the church for more than fifteen years and had become rather weary and passive with his pastoral duties. The church's board of directors, on which Bob was serving at the time, voted to release the pastor from his duties. The problem then arose as to where we would find a pastor who wanted to move to our remote area and pastor a church with the majority of the congregation being more than sixty years old and no children.

It was common for guests to visit our church since Nocona Hills is a golfing/retirement community located on a lake. The residents are always curious about what brings people to our remote area. The congregation immediately noticed a couple who were guests one Sunday morning. After visiting with the couple, we learned they were from the Dallas area, the man worked as an estate planner, and his wife, a musician and teacher. He told us he had a client who owned a small house in Nocona Hills, and given that the man's family did not want the house, he offered to give it to the couple. They accepted the gift and were excited because they thought it would be a nice weekend retreat from the city. The couple was warmly welcomed to our congregation in the way God receives anyone into His family.

As some of us spoke to our visitors, it was explained to them we were between pastors. I am not sure why we were surprised when the man revealed to us he had been in the ministry during his military service and could fill in for us as a substitute preacher until we found someone permanent. Without hesitation, the church members accepted his offer. The next week he began preaching, and his beautiful wife blessed our congregation with the most amazing worship music I had ever heard.

Our temporary pastor's dynamic, animated talent of delivering a sermon, along with his wife's passionate musical gifts, increased the attendance in our church each week. Before long, we were placing folding chairs in the aisles on the old, lime green carpet. Couples, both young and old, were coming from miles away to attend and with them they brought their children, many children. The couple worked lovingly to build a children and youth program. Church volunteers began picking up enthusiastic kids in the area and delivering them to church on Sundays and Wednesday nights. It was almost as if someone had staged this biblical intervention. I wonder who that could have been—God perhaps!

It was soon apparent we needed more space. An architect in our church graciously offered his expertise and prepared plans for a 200-seat sanctuary, and the building was soon constructed. Our rapidly increasing membership caught the eye of local newspapers, and a full page was devoted to the incredible growth of our small country church. God was performing His amazing work as only He could do.

Before the building construction was complete, the board approached me with an offer to become secretary for the church. After praying about this, I accepted the position, knowing this was where God wanted me. The Bible states God knows our plans before we are conceived in our mother's womb. I didn't have to toil over my decision this time. God gave me my answer, and it was obvious all the factors were perfectly aligned.

As I reflect now, it is almost eerie to recognize that from the time I attended high school, I wanted to work in the secretarial and accounting field, and I attended college with that specific goal in mind. I had been employed as a secretary since I was nineteen years old. I worked for the infamous Hunt family in an administrative position in downtown Dallas. For several years, I worked as an administrative assistant for a wealthy Dallas oil baron who owned what is now a major part of the city of Addison, land around DFW airport, and a large racing and breeding quarter horse ranch near Denton. I had more than twenty-five years experience in the secular world, but never in a church ministry position. I knew I could easily perform the clerical duties involved, but I knew the ministry aspect would definitely be a challenge.

A few weeks after becoming church secretary, I was invited to San Antonio to attend my first Women of Faith National Conference. Fifteen thousand women filled the Alamo Dome, and as you can imagine, the noise was deafening! I was privileged to listen to some of the most amazing Christian women speakers and musicians. Among those on the agenda were Luci Swindoll, Marilyn Meberg, Patsy Clairmont, Sheila Walsh, and Nicole C. Mullins. The conference proved a most inspirational, emotional Christian experience for me. For four days, we shared tears, laughter, and song. This was definitely a major life changing Christian experiences for me. I praise God that I was blessed to attend.

My friends and I shared a hotel suite on the San Antonio River Walk. We stayed up all hours of the nights sharing stories, laughing, and crying. We shared our life experiences and talked about how God had changed each of our lives. I felt something once again that I could not explain. God had entered into my life in a different way that week, through my girlfriends and fifteen thousand other women I didn't know. I witnessed the strong faith exhibited by many women who had God in their lives.

Women from all walks of life publically demonstrated their faith, and I saw how joyfully full of pride they were to be Christians. I grasped a concept I had been missing for so many years of my life. I knew God personally, but I had unknowingly shied away from a public demonstration of my love for Him. I returned home with a very different, improved mindset. I would now feel comfortable about sharing my faith with others. At my request, God had become an integral part of my life, and from this point on, I would be proud to reveal my faith to anyone willing to listen, and even to those who weren't. That week, God trained me to serve in a ministry position. Our church continued to grow and prosper with a full congregation each Sunday, my responsibilities became more and more demanding, but I loved every minute of it! This was definitely my calling and how God intended for me to serve Him.

Bob too became more involved in the church, and he continued to support me in my new endeavor. He found his calling to serve in so many ways he had not recognized before. It is sometimes difficult for people to understand how even the smallest thing you do for your church is a gift from and for God. Everyone can serve God, whether it's folding bulletins on Friday afternoon, washing dirty windows instead of complaining about them, or singing in the choir or praise team. By simply picking up trash in the parking lot, arranging flowers for the pulpit, pulling weeds in the flowerbeds, or greeting people at the door, know your church needs you! Do not ever believe you do not have a gift to offer your church. God has given us everything, and everything we have is to be used for His glory, so use it.

I look back now and realize that before I became the church secretary, I had not recognized the pure gratification of serving my God. No other position I held throughout my life gave me the satisfaction I received from working for God and His church. It wasn't even something I would qualify as work; it was so rewarding it did not seem like a job. I began counseling and helping people in my new ministry. I began telling others about what God had done for me through my own life experiences. I was a living example of the power of God. I would no longer withdraw from my past or ignore what God wanted me to share. He had never given up on me, and He waited patiently knowing someday I would recognize everything I am, and everything I have I owe to Him.

~~~

Unfortunately, as in the secular world, differences of opinion become a struggle for power even within a church. Look back in the book of Revelation and review the letters God instructed Paul to write to the seven churches. Almost every church is admonished for one reason or another. Throughout time, members have left one church for another due to a difference of opinion. People leave, people return, and sometimes they even develop their own new churches only to discover there is no difference. Why? Because there is no perfect church! People make up churches, and there are no perfect people, so there will never be a perfect church on this earth.

The power struggles in a church may be an opinion about something as insignificant as the songs our church sings, how our buildings are to be used, or how our money is being spent. The key word here is *our*. Nothing in a church is *ours*, not the money in the bank or the buildings. God doesn't care what words we sing, what tempo is used or what instruments are played, as long as we are worshiping Him. Nothing is ours; it all belongs to God! I believe, until this concept is understood, a church cannot succeed. Certainly, God expects us to be good stewards of the things of the church, but our only responsibility for these things is to manage them and make sure they are used solely for the glory of His name to expand further His Word to others.

I have come to believe the primary purpose of the church is to fellowship and worship with other believers. But to me, more importantly church is a key medium for learning, to prepare us, building up our spiritual strength so we can go outside the church building, outside our comfort zones, outside the box so to speak, to reach others who don't know Him. This is what I believe God intended His church to be, not a building, but an invisible structure of unity among His believers. I am not implying that I think God wants us to become like the "Jesus freak" we see on the intersections in our cities who rants and raves about repenting or we will go to hell, or maybe He does? I don't know. What I do know is God wants us to go out into the world and live a life that reflects His grace and teaches others about His amazing love. That, to me, is God's church.

Through my studies, I have come to believe the church unit was developed to share the gospel with everyone, not just our friends who are easy to love, but the less fortunate, the children, the unbelievers, and yes, even the people we may not like. The church is literally our relationship with God.

From time to time, Satan will raise his ugly head and through his powers working within a church, he will attempt to destroy God's work. When this happens, I've seen a sense of despair fall upon a church. Financial worries become an issue even though God has always provided every dollar needed. When this happens, outreach seems to become the first ministry to receive cuts, and the despair becomes a "let's take care of ourselves first, and then we will reach out to others." Outreach will not support a church financially, and it will often seem there is only a hand-out mentality, and all we are doing is giving. But isn't that what God's love and His church are all about? If a church doesn't reach out to others through its programs and teach those who do not know God, the church will die.

An outreach ministry is similar to performing a random act of kindness, the pay it forward effect. "Give and you will receive. Your gift will return to you in full—pressed down, shaken together to make room for more, running over, and poured into your lap. The amount you give will determine the amount you get back." I believe this scripture in Luke 6:38 does not refer to monetary giving alone. It can also apply to a church that reaches out to teach others God's Word, bringing unbelievers to Christ, regardless of where they live, their background, age or financial status.

~~~

Four years into my ministry, I felt a disconcerting development within our church; Satan was prowling. Concerns about finances began mounting within the church. Soon staffing changes were made and ministry programs were slashed to save money. There was a sudden sense of urgency emerging, which focused on paying off the already significantly reduced building construction loan. It was obvious the progressive mindsets of many had taken an unexpected downward spiral. I soon learned of the decision to cut costs by outsourcing many elements of my ministry. I wanted to believe God was not finished with me in my church, but I soon realized my services was not wanted any longer and my purpose had been completed. I was crushed, disappointed, and heartbroken.

It took some time before God set me free from the disappointment I felt when I was no longer needed in a position where God had placed me. However, God soon demonstrated to me that I could follow and embrace Him and His work more deeply in other areas of my life. Through pastor's inspirational teachings and the Holy Spirit working within me, I had been blessed to abundantly learn about God and His plans for me. I became increasingly motivated to share my testimony with others.

Within a few weeks of leaving my position at the church, Bob received an unsolicited job offer. We instinctively knew God had arranged for this and without hesitation, Bob accepted the offer. The position would require travel, and now I would be able to be with him. We began to travel extensively once again, but this time, we felt we had a different mission. Our lives became a platform for our ministry emphasizing the wondrous works of God. We recognized God wanted us to be exposed to His Word in different regions and other churches. In doing this we were allowed to learn so much and share testimonies with many. We gained knowledge and felt even more moved by the power of God.

Pastor had continually encouraged me to write a book about my life. Through his own missionary experiences, he explained how this would provide me a greater opportunity to spread the Word of God through my testimony. I was flattered he believed my story was worth sharing, but it took some time before I attempted to author a book. When I first began writing, it was about me. As a result, the words did not come, and I struggled for several months. I made the decision I would have to reconsider the effort involved to write an entire book.

When Bob and I arrived at our Colorado summer home, I took a walk deep into the forest. I had always felt an unexplainable closeness to God and His world in this particular area. It is a place of peace for me, a place where I can hear God speaking through the quietness. As I sat alongside the meandering creek among the towering spruce trees, I looked up at the majestic mountaintops. I began meditating and talking with Him. There in the midst of God's marvelous works, I prayed fervently and aloud. I prayed to God, I pleaded with Him. If He wanted me to write a book, He would have to give me the words. As I walked back to our home, I somehow knew I would write a book, but it would not be about me. It would be about God. How He had used my family, friends, and me for His works.

A few days later, Bob was called away from Colorado on business, and I sat alone at my computer and began to write. I wrote for hours every day, typing as fast as I could, the words flowing through me with unimaginable speed. I felt God was speaking through me. I knew then He had answered my prayers. I was doing what He wanted me to do, saying what He wanted me to say. I was following His direction as I had been trained to do, and He would make its purpose successful.

~~~

My faith made me certain of realities I could not see. I can't see the wind, but I feel it, I may not be able to see the sun on a certain day because of the clouds, but I know it remains in the sky, I feel its warmth, God's warmth. Faith had become a strong force in my life, a force to be used for God's glory. It's as if I can hear Him saying to me, "Be still, listen to Me, I am not finished with you. I still have many more plans for you." Faith gave me the courage to trust that I am doing the work God has for me.

The phase of my life when I worked in my church ministry prepared me even more to accept His plans. During our travels, I have had the courage and privilege to give my testimony to a number of small groups. I reflect to my college days and what I thought at the time was the worse class I could have imagined in my young life, Public Speaking! I now presume God even had my college class schedule in mind for my future. Why is it that the things He planned for me continue to surprise me?

All my life I had worked for others, and I served others including myself. It wasn't until I found my true God and His purpose for me in that little yellow metal building with lime green carpet in Nocona Hills. As most of us do, I took much of His plan for granted. I treasured He was with me through tragedy, and I treasured the new life experiences He had given me. But I now know He is definitely not finished with me. I can feel the wind I cannot see. I feel I should brace myself, for He is thrusting a powerful force beneath my wings!

CHAPTER 17

This Little Light of Mine

And God saw that the light was good.
Then he separated the light from the darkness.
—Genesis 1:4

It has been proven that a normal person has about fifty thousand thoughts a day, that's a lot of thinking! It is also said that 90 percent of these thoughts are the same ones we had the day before. What a waste of our time! Every single thought we have is either good or bad! Our actions are originated through our thoughts. The decisions I made in my life defines who I am as a person. God has graciously allowed me to react to my own thoughts; thus I have authority over my actions.

When a thought surfaces in my mind, it comes from either God or Satan. To visualize this, I imagine an angel (God) sitting on my right shoulder, on my left a devil (Satan) sits, and in the center is my head where my decisions are culminated. God allows me to make the decision as to which one I will choose. In order for me to think good and pleasant thoughts, I have to make the right choices; I have to choose God's side. If I will continually allow God into my thought process, I am filled with His goodness and there is no room remaining for Satan. When God fills my mind, He in turn fills my heart and I am blessed beyond imagination, releasing me to live a joy-filled life.

Throughout times in my life I lived in the flesh, I searched for happiness and joy in the wrong places. I eventually found that material things were not what made me happy. I discovered every single day, every thought I had gave me the opportunity to decide whether or not I would be joyful. There is joy in everything and everyone; I just had to look to find it.

I confess I have frequent conversations with myself. People say you are crazy only if you answer yourself. Well, I hate to admit it, but I may be right on that edge! In the conversations, I have concluded I'm actually conversing with God, who continually shapes my future one thought at a time. I cannot even imagine what my thought process would be like if I absolutely, completely trusted God. For us, as humans, is this even possible? I say I trust God, but do I completely trust Him? I am implying a trust so powerful that I believe no one has really ever felt such authority. I'm talking about the kind of trust Jesus Christ had for His Father as He was nailed to the cross. I can't even imagine that distinction of trust. I attempt to have it by living in constant conversation with God and making good decisions, but I am sure I fall so extremely short of it. However, I believe all God wants us to do, is to try! He knows our hearts.

After experiencing the devastation in my life, I continually strive to live in this trust and peace. I had lived a happy, joyful life with my husband and children, but that life is gone forever except in my thoughts. I have memories of things that were pleasant and now bring me joy; I have memories of the difficult times Larry and I experienced as a young couple, and those thoughts bring me sadness. So which ones do I choose to remember? The pleasant thoughts, of course! The choice I make every day is to live in joy and happiness, not doom and gloom. As I experience happiness, joy will then fill my heart.

I have known people who do not live in the present. How often do we express that our future will be better, "when this or that happens" or "when I retire"? God doesn't want us to live in the past or the future, He expects us to live with Him in the present. The present is a gift from Him. "This is the day the Lord has made. We will rejoice and be glad in it." (Psalm 118:24) The Bible does not say yesterday or tomorrow, it says today! There were days when the last thing I wanted to do was to rejoice, my sorrow was overwhelming. On those days, I discovered if I spoke to God and told Him truly how I felt, how sad I was, He would always show me reasons to rejoice and be glad. This thought is continued throughout the Bible, and the apostle Paul tells the church of Philippi in Philippians 4:4, "Always be full of joy in the Lord. I say it again---rejoice!" He says it a total of sixteen times in four chapters, so I think he believed what he said.

The Old Testament book of Job tells the story of Job, a man of God who lived a gripping drama of riches-to-rags-to-riches yet his faith endured through it all. In Job 3:25, Job says, "What I always feared happened to me. What I dreamed has come true." Jesus says throughout the Bible that we are in essence, the result of "what we believe." If I had decided to feel sorry for myself, I would have been disobedient and disrespectful to God. God gave me everything I am. If I had chosen to live a wretched life, I would be saying "God gave me this wretched life to live." Humans took away my family, but God continued to give me everything I needed to be joyous, so how could I live otherwise if I trusted Him!

The apostle Paul challenges us in Philippians, to seek out and dwell on the positives in our lives. Once I found those places, I realized they are in the presence of God. In essence, Paul is telling us what I have been trying to explain, we always have a choice. We can listen to Satan on our left shoulder, or we can live the joy-filled life by following the instructions of the angel on our right side, God!

Unfortunately, simply following God's instructions will not always make us happy. God tells us to do the things that

139

are good, and let's admit, we don't always want to do what's good. He looks at the positive, and that is where my focus needs to be. We must remember to always find a positive in the negatives, none of that "stinking thinking"! If I had chosen to consider myself a victim, I would never have been victorious over the depressing areas in my life.

My husband, Bob, has always been an encouraging influence in my life. From the day he told me to "take my life one day at a time," to the present, he has managed to help me stay focused on the positive. I never had a dominating negative attitude, but there were always times when a little pessimism would creep into my life. If I make a comment to Bob that the meteorologist is forecasting a 70 percent chance of rain tomorrow, Bob will tell me that means there is a 30 percent chance it won't rain! I jokingly tell him I hate it when he is so positive. But actually, he helps me focus on the positive things I want to happen, and invariably positive things happen!

As I've aged and try to work on an intricate task, I often have difficulty focusing my eyesight on a project. I've got to find my glasses, or even worse, a magnifying glass! I simply cannot see the project as clearly as I should. Even though I've been given the gift of sight, and it may not be as sharp as it use to be, I can still see with some aid. I must continue to focus on the positive. I have the sight, now all I need is a light.

Have you ever been working on a project when someone else is holding the flashlight for you? It can be so very frustrating because the person never seems to point the light exactly where you need to see. Don't you think God probably feels the same way with us sometimes? I've reached up and grabbed the hand holding the light, and instructed that person to hold it right where I want them to, but they will always let the beam drift away again. Can't you just imagine God wanting to shake us sometimes and tell us to do as He directs. Then we would be able to see His path. So simple! As in life, we must find our own glasses and aim our own flashlight where God wants us. Aim your light in the right direction so you can see the target. Aim it toward God. Don't allow yourself to focus on the darkness or the negative surrounding you, don't say, "I just can't see as well as I used to." Be thankful God has given us the eyes we have and that we can direct what little sight we have towards God.

I learned early on that I could not focus on losing my children. I was blessed to have given birth twice, to nurse my crying, sleepy babies, and to care for them throughout the little time I had to spend with them. I will not allow myself to dwell on the things taken away from me. I was blessed with good eyesight during their lives, and once my sight was taken away, I now see their lives through my memories. I refuse to live in the blindness of the past; I live in the present and joyfully reminisce, because I made that choice. God created us to be joyful in spirit, and true joy is a sign of our faith in God. I am not happy about losing my children, but I remain joyful, there is a huge difference. Happiness is what I felt in the flesh when my children were alive with me, joyful is what I feel spiritually! God has given me memories to see my past, spiritual eyes to see my future, and I work to keep both healthy and living.

Sometimes, when I'm holding the flashlight in my hand, I have to remind myself to pull it back a little and enlarge my circle of light; to see more of the world around me. There is much more out there than the task on which I allow myself to focus. God's true vision should not be limited to my eyes only, so I want to try to shed some light on the path of deeper spiritual realms. My eyes of faith, my spiritual eyes, can see through the darkness that surrounds me. When I focus on the positive, I am assisting others to see Him better, I am serving God's purpose. Be the light for someone else in your life and help him or her focus on the positive. Help them to see His light more clearly. You will be blessed abundantly if you shine His light for someone else.

CHAPTER 18

My Faith Made Me Well

Trust the Lord with all your heart,
and don't depend on your own understanding.
—Proverbs 3:5

I have found myself in the season of my life where God laid upon my heart the inspiration to write this book. The primary purpose of this endeavor is to pass on to others how God will bless each of you if you simply ask for His assistance and guidance and be willing to submit to His direction. This unprecedented undertaking in my life was something I did not take lightly. I have related stories to you about the many exciting and enjoyable times Bob and I have experienced in our lives together. However, it is very important for me to emphasize that I did not write of these experiences to make an impression or boast. I merely wanted to express how material things did not satisfy me. It wasn't until my faith matured that I recognized how God remained with me the entire time. He patiently waited until I grew to Him spiritually. I did not realize during all those experiences that He continued to bless me.

Someone once remarked to me that I must surely relate to the story of Job in the Old Testament. At the time, I had to reread Job's story to refresh my memory, and I could then easily understand the comparison of our similar circumstances. Job's story and the tragedies he experienced troubles many people, making them wonder how God would allow such things to happen to His own, good people. At one time, I wondered that myself.

The essence of Job's story is that throughout all the terribly difficult times he experienced, he was never tempted to give up his faith even though his friends tried to convince him it was God causing his suffering. There were people around me who assumed that what I went through was something God had planned all along. I could not and refused not to accept their assumptions.

It is impossible for me to explain how I was able to continue to trust God after the wreck and throughout my recovery. I do believe, however, it was that "tiny mustard seed of faith" planted in me as a child, which provided me with just enough knowledge to know God had not caused my suffering and that He was there to help me. As I lay in the crumpled metal of our vehicle, I knew in every depth of my soul, at that very moment, my family lay around me dying. I could do nothing except use the only diminutive source of energy I had left, a prayer to my Father!

The God I knew could not and did not plan to kill my innocent family and place me in such anguish. The simple fact is God does not cause terrible things to happen to His children. God, in His infinite wisdom, placed us on this earth as humans designed in His likeness. He gave us free will, which allows us to make our own decisions. This is precisely why we sin and make mistakes; we are human, not perfect like God. If I had believed God caused the wreck due to some divine plan He had for us, I most likely would have loathed Him and wanted to die myself that day. Dying would have certainly been the easy way out for me. I would not have had to experience the suffering, mourning, injuries, or loneliness I endured.

God was there for me when I needed Him. Don't misunderstand me, I did not intend to "wait until I needed Him" to call out for His help. But in my busy, self-absorbed life, I made the unfortunate choice to live without Him and His help. He is such an awesome God. Even though I chose to ignore Him at times, He continued to stand beside me. What a faithful love. Through His mercy, He gave me the opportunity to call out for His help, with a no questions asked policy.

Did I feel anger when I suffered my loss? Of course I did! After all, I am human, and God allowed me the choice to be angry. But because I had called out for His help, the feeling I had was anger toward the situation in which human beings had placed me, not a situation God created. I called out to my Father, not in a rage, but in a sacrificial way in supplication for His help. There was no one else who could have helped me survive my enormous loss and injuries. God instantaneously took over my spirit and my life when I called to Him. It was as if He said to me, "Take my hand, child. I will guide you through one day at a time, and I will never leave your side if you will only allow me to live within you."

If I had chosen to live my life with anger and rage toward the world and everyone involved, I almost certainly would have lived a miserable, bitter life without God. He allowed me to choose to be angry at the world. I was angry and enraged at the man who made the poor choice of drinking and driving. I was angry because I will not witness my children growing up. I will never see Cliff play football or help Adrianne select her wedding dress. Larry and I would never be blessed to enjoy our grandchildren. Even through all these disappointments, my God gave me the capacity for forgiveness to release my anger toward this world and turn to His perfect justice system for satisfaction.

The suffering I went through was not what made me strong. I gained the strength and power to survive from the Holy Spirit the moment I called out for His help. Through His amazing power, He gave me strength, both emotional and spiritual. God gave me a power that I cannot explain in everyday language or gain by earthly means. Through God's mercy, He has made this gift available to everyone. All we have to do is ask for it. Throughout the Bible, God never promises us a life free from pain and suffering. As humans, I know we are going to suffer, but God is always there for us to draw upon for our strength and courage.

Job's friends kept asking him to repent for the secret sins he surely committed to have received such suffering, and he did eventually ask for forgiveness. Ironically, Job's repentance was for his sin of questioning God's sovereignty and justice. If I had angrily asked how God could let such a tragedy happen, I would have had to have the humility to admit I didn't have enough faith to trust God's goodness. When God gave me the strength, I mustered enough faith to trust Him. Only then did He begin answering my prayers.

Assuming Job must have sinned, his friends judged him, just as I am sure there were those who judged my family thinking that what had happened was a result of what they perceived to be our sinful lives. I know Larry and I did not live perfect lives, but God did not allow their deaths because of our sin. The Bible instructs us to be careful not to judge others because they are experiencing misfortune in their lives. Even today, sin left un-confessed and the failure of faith are blamed for disease and the lack of material blessings. This debate may last forever, "Why does God allow suffering and trouble to affect His people?" God is and always will be in control. Still, in our world, both the good and bad people will always be plagued by sin, tragedy, and suffering because of our human decisions, our choices.

Throughout my life, I had been exposed to the information that God was there for me, to protect me. Yet, it took a disaster in my life to make me truly experience God and His goodness. If you take away only one thing from this book, let me say to you, do not wait for a disaster to enjoy the wonderful life God has available for everyone. Prior to the wreck, I never really took the time to get to know God. I never sat down to read the Bible or meditate on scriptures. God wants us to do more than just read His book; He wants us to learn from it. He doesn't expect us to sit down and read the Bible from cover to cover so we can boast and say, "I've read the entire Bible." God wanted me to know Him, just as I did my spouse or a dear, close friend, and the only way I could do this was to apply the lessons found in the Bible. This is how I truly came to know God and make Him my friend. Things take time, especially good things, like developing a strong, enduring friendship. There is a saying, "A good friend is one who really knows you and still likes you." I want to have this kind of relationship with God. He knows me and will always love me. What a genuine friendship!

Knowing and learning about God is not a simple task, it will take time and endurance. Look at ants, tiny creatures God created, and observe the monumental tasks they accomplish. They build huge mounds of a city by moving tiny grains of sand one at a time. They pick up a piece of sand and take that first step, then the next, and the next. This is exactly what God expects from us, to take one tiny grain at a time, and then one day at a time we build our faith and trust in Him. He knows what can be accomplished if we will approach our life in this respect.

All of these instructions seem to come full circle. I learned I would never know God unless I experienced Him, and I couldn't experience Him unless I knew Him personally. I had to learn to know what He expected, know what to ask, and know how to tell others about Him. Follow the instruction book, the Bible. It has to be studied every single day to keep us in constant conversation with God.

Romans 5:11 tells us, "The closer you are to God, the less you consider yourself …" The life experiences I have been through made me different and less selfish. The experiences have made me a much more sensitive, caring, and loving person, and God has granted me the gift of compassion and discernment. Throughout my church ministry, He developed me into a sympathetic counselor. God was molding me, just as a potter would shape clay. He taught me understand people better and their feelings. I learned to feel their pain and comfort them. I learned the art of forgiveness, a truly treasured gift with which God blessed me at a time I desperately needed it. I am a more complete person now, but not because of the tragedy, but because of the things I learned from God beginning on that hot July day in 1986. Would I trade all the knowledge and spiritual growth to have my family back? I pray I will never be in a position to have to answer that question.

What I do know is, because of my spiritual growth I gained during the tragedy, one day my family and I will reunite. That is all the promise I need to continue serving and worshiping my God. I know a different God now than I did before that fateful day. I am confident He will always be with me. Since the day I met Him early in my teen years, He has been near my side and reaching for my hand as we walked together down the path of my life. All I had to do was reach up, take His hand, and He would position each of my steps.

Sometimes, I wanted to believe my own willpower made me strong, and maybe God had given me the strength so I wouldn't need to depend on Him so much. Nothing could be farther from the truth. I fell into that trap for years during my recovery, but thankfully, I recognized the emptiness and reached up to grab His hand once again. It is so easy to slip away from Him; don't let this happen to you.

God will give us a spiritual rebirth simply by asking, but I wish it were that easy. It's a long, slow, difficult journey, and one that I have begun to make. Like the ants, I carry those grains of sand that represent my faith. I drop them, go back, pick them up again, and retrace my steps. But each time I dropped my faith, I did not take the same path. I learned from my mistakes, and I feel I am closer to my goal of getting to know God better. He will be there waiting for me, reaching out for me to take His hand so He can help me over another hurdle.

As I sit here today, more than twenty-five years after the loss of my family, I am able to reflect on my past, and I realize how much time I wasted by not experiencing a stronger relationship with God. Would my life have been different? I don't know. What I do know is that the day He needed me to serve Him, I realized everything I am and everything I will ever be, I owed to Him. I am content in this season of my life with God. As Paul told the Philippians, "I have lived on almost nothing and have lived with everything, for I can do everything through Christ, who gives me strength." (Phillipians 4:12) I learned to live with what I had, not always wanting for something, and I became satisfied. God will supply our every need, but not according to our desire, but in the way He knows is best for us.

I learned to treasure every moment. I treasured my family, my parents and my friends. We do not have the gift of knowing how long we will have these precious lives on earth. The day of the wreck began as any other day in my life, but in the blink of an eye, my family was gone and my life changed forever. I am so grateful for the short time I had to spend with Larry, Cliff, and Adrianne. There is not a single thing in this world that can take away the precious memories I hold so close to my heart. Not a day passes that I do not have a thought about them, for they will always live in my heart while wrapped in the loving arms of God.

In Luke 8:45-48, an unruly crowd in a local synagogue surrounded Jesus. There, a suffering, bleeding woman fought through the crowd. Her faith was so strong she knew if she could merely touch the hem of His garment, she would be healed. Coming up behind Jesus, she only touched the fringe of His robe. Jesus said, "Who touched me? Someone deliberately touched me, for I felt healing power go out from me." I expect, I too, would have begun to tremble and fall to my knees in front of him and try to explain as this woman did. Jesus answered me just as He said to her, "Daughter, your faith has made you well. Go in peace."

In Loving Memory
of

Larry Marlon Hill
November 14, 1953 – July 5, 1986

Clifton Marlon Hill
October 24, 1975 – July 5, 1986

Adrianne Marie Hill
May 19, 1978 – July 5, 1986

CPSIA information can be obtained at www.ICGtesting.com
Printed in the USA
LVOW122339040912

297366LV00001B/1/P